RATIO ANALYSIS

RATIO ANALYSIS

Michael F. Morley, BA, FCA
Professor of Accountancy
University of Aberdeen

This monograph is published in the Research Advisory Committee of the Institute of Chartered Accountants of Scotland and does not necessarily represent the views of the Research Advisory Committee or of the Council of the Institute.

No responsibility for loss occasioned to any person acting or refraining from action as a result of any material in this publication can be accepted by the author or publisher.

All rights reserved. No part of this publication may be reproduced, stored in a retrieval system, or transmitted, in any form or by any means, electronic, mechanical, photocopying, recording or otherwise, without the prior permission of the publisher.

A version first published in 1984 by
Van Nostrand Reinhold (UK) Co. Ltd.,
Molly Millars Lane, Wokingham, Berkshire, England

Reprinted 1992

Published for the Council, June 1984
Gee Publishing Ltd., Fetter Lane, London WC1 0BU

Printed in Great Britain

British Library Cataloguing in Publication Data

Morley, M. F.
    Ratio analysis.
    (Accountancy)
    1. Ratio analysis 2. Institute of Chartered
    Accountants of Scotland. The Institute
    3. 657.48151984 2. 657   I. Series
    HF5681.R25   0-85258-233-6   657.3 5681

ISBN 0-85258-233-6

Published for
THE INSTITUTE OF CHARTERED
ACCOUNTANTS OF SCOTLAND
by
GEE & CO (PUBLISHERS) LIMITED

A Gee text first published in 1984 by
Van Nostrand Reinhold (UK) Co. Ltd
Molly Millars Lane, Wokingham, Berkshire, England

Reprinted 1985

Photoset in 9 on 11 point Times by
Kelly Typesetting Ltd, Bradford-on-Avon, Wiltshire
Printed in Hong Kong

Library of Congress Cataloging in Publication Data

Morley, M. F.
  Ratio analysis.
  Bibliography: p.
  1. Ratio analysis. I. Institute of Chartered
Accountants of Scotland. II. Title.
HF5681.R25M631984   657'.33   83—21818
ISBN 0—85258—233—1

Foreword

This series of monographs has been initiated by the Research Advisory Committee of The Institute of Chartered Accountants of Scotland. The Committee believes that, at a time both of change and of increasing interest in accounting information, these monographs will meet a need for clear explanation of some of the more difficult concepts relevant to the preparation of corporate accounting reports. All are written by acknowledged experts in their respective fields in a style which will appeal equally to the specialist and the well informed general reader. Some will be relevant to the needs of one group more than another, but they are addressed principally to accountants, bankers, civil servants, directors, financial journalists, investment managers, investment analysts, private investors, managers, trade union officials and others with an interest in accounting information. Opinions expressed by the authors are, of course, their own.

Contents

Preface   vii

Introduction   ix

1 Ratios Measuring Profitability and Performance   1
   Return on capital   1
   Profit to sales   4
   Sales to capital   7
   Value added to sales   10
   Value added to payroll costs   12
   Earnings per share   13

2 Ratios Measuring Liquidity, Solvency and Financial Structure   15
   Current ratio   16
   Liquid asset ratio   19
   Debtors turnover   20
   Stock turnover   21
   Gearing ratio   23
   Interest cover ratio   27

3 Ratios Derived from Consolidated Accounts   30
   Overseas subsidiaries   31
   Merger accounting   33
   Associate companies   33

4 The Dangers of Ratio Analysis   35
   Accounting policies   35
   Peculiarities of the trade   36
   Improper comparisons   39
   Technical errors   40
   Exclusive reliance on ratios   41

Appendix   44
   Illustrations of the construction of ratios from the accounts of
   Scottish and Newcastle Breweries   44

Further Reading on Ratio Analysis   53

Preface

Many of those who look at the accounts of businesses will at some stage have experienced a feeling of inadequacy. "Where do I begin, now that I am faced with this mass of detailed information?" "What is the meaning of all these figures; how should I interpret them?" The use of ratio analysis can be a first step towards correcting this situation.

Ratio analysis is the term used for the process of calculating and appraising financial ratios extracted from the accounts of a business. Each ratio expresses the relationship between a pair of numbers taken from the balance sheet and/or the profit statement. Examples are the ratio of profit to capital employed and the ratio of current assets to current liabilities. The point of using such ratios is twofold. First, they compress the extensive detail of the accounts to understandable proportions, thereby saving time and avoiding the danger of information overload. Second, they guide the user towards asking the right questions and making better business decisions.

The proposition that ratio analysis improves decision making is supported by evidence of two sorts. First, ratios have grown steadily in popularity through the twentieth century (having been very little used before 1900) and this popularity has grown amongst practical men who have had to live with the consequences of their decisions. Second, the availability of computer facilities has enabled researchers to calculate large numbers of ratios for large numbers of companies over many years. This data has then been compared with information as to which companies have gone into liquidation or defaulted on loans. Generally this research has confirmed the usefulness of ratios as tests for discriminating between businesses with satisfactory financial positions and those heading for failure. Quite often, however, the researchers have not ranked the ratios in the same order of usefulness as does the current conventional wisdom of accountants. These research projects have been surveyed by Foster.[1]

In what follows, the ratios have been given roughly the degree of emphasis

[1]   Foster, G. "Financial Statement Analysis", Prentice Hall, 1978.

accorded them by conventional wisdom rather than by the empirical research studies. This is partly because almost all the research results relate to American companies in the 1960s and 1970s, whilst the economic environment of European companies in the 1980s seems to be very different. Also, this choice has been made because the research into ratios as predictors of business failure has typically used vast quantities of data but has rather ignored theory, in that the models tested have had low theoretical content and have contributed little to the state of theory. This brute empiricism has not therefore helped ratio users understand why some companies fail and some prosper.

The coverage of this monograph has deliberately been limited to the use of ratios in financial accounting; their use in management accounting is not discussed. This treatment of ratios is therefore of relevance to those "outside" the business, whether investors or lenders, who are appraising it, using its annual accounts. The discussion is not directly concerned with the "insiders" who are responsible for the day-to-day management of the business. Furthermore, the coverage is in general concerned with the accounts of a company, though it normally applies also to a firm carried on by an individual or in partnership. A separate section reviews the special factors involved when judging the ratios of a group of companies.

I am deeply indebted to the members of the Research Advisory Committee of The Institute of Chartered Accountants of Scotland, and to colleagues at the University of Aberdeen, for many helpful comments and suggestions on earlier drafts. Responsibility for all remaining faults is my own, as are the opinions expressed, which are not necessarily shared by those who have helped me.

M. F. Morley
University of Aberdeen
1983

Introduction

Ratio analysis is useful to virtually all readers of financial accounting statements. The two main categories of readers will be investors in and lenders to the company. The investor group will be the shareholders and potential shareholders in a company and the lenders will comprise actual and potential providers of loans, including overdrafts and trade credit. The investors will concentrate therefore on profitability and performance ratios, since the point of investing in a company is to increase one's income and/or wealth, and profits are the source of this increase, whilst the lender category of ratio user will concentrate on the ratios which measure liquidity, solvency and risk. There is some crossover of interest in these categories of user (and of ratio), since the investor does have an interest in his company's liquidity and the lender does have some interest in profitability. However, these interests are subordinate to the main ones, which are the investor's desire to maximise his profits and the lender's desire for certainty as to the interest and capital repayments due to him.

There are other relationships with the company, apart from that of investor or lender, which will give rise to an interest in the company's accounting ratios. For example, employees of the company, and their representatives in trade unions, will be able to use ratios as a preliminary guide to the likelihood of continued secure employment and the ability to afford pay increases. Also, the suppliers to the company, together with its customers, can use the company's ratios to assess whether future trading links are in jeopardy. Various government officials may use ratios to help them make decisions about the company: tax gatherers can judge the reasonableness of data supplied to them, and monopoly-regulation officials can judge whether the company dominates its market and how it uses its power. The auditor of the company will generally use ratios as an aid to understanding its trading pattern and uncovering reasons for any changes.

None of these ratio-using groups should rely exclusively on ratios, but each group will be helped by ratio analysis, which often provides a good starting point for marshalling information needed for business decisions. The various users of ratios may be generating predictions (*eg*, that the company will meet its obligations on time) and may be deciding upon courses of action (*eg*, an increase in an overdraft limit) largely on the strength of the ratios themselves and of how these ratios compare with other businesses and with preconceived rules of thumb as to what is "healthy" for a given ratio.

There are two ways in which this discussion of ratios departs from convention. First, much more attention than is usual is given to ratios based on current cost accounting (in the version of CCA defined by SSAP 16)[1]. Second, the emphasis given to ratios using value added (VA) is greater than most accountants would give, but is probably in accordance with the importance of VA in the eyes of most businessmen.

The following discussion begins with the two main users of financial ratios, starting with the measurement of profitability and performance and moving on to the measurement of liquidity, solvency and financial structure. There is then a review of the special factors which are involved when ratios are extracted from the consolidated accounts of a group of companies rather than from the accounts of a single company. This is followed by a section which points out the dangers of ratio analysis and how these may be guarded against. The final section is a worked example, showing how ratios are derived from an actual set of accounts.

[1] ASC: Statement of Standard Accounting Practice No 16 Current Cost accounting, March 1980.

1 Ratios Measuring Profitability and Performance

Every business in the private sector of the economy must, in the long run, be profitable if it is to survive. Profitability is necessary if investors and lenders are to continue to support the business. However, profitabilty cannot be assessed simply by considering the annual profit figure. The current annual profits of a multi-national oil company may be £1,000 million, while those of a small family company may be only £10,000. By themselves these figures tell us little about whether the companies are well run, are worth investing in or even whether they are likely to continue trading for the foreseeable future. To make judgments on these matters we need to relate the profits to other accounting magnitudes. A first step is to relate profit to the resources invested in the company, thereby revealing the return on capital.

Return on capital

To construct this ratio, the net profit, which measures the net return available for shareholders, is divided by the shareholders' funds. To be more precise, the numerator is the net profit after interest, taxation and minority interests. The reason for taking the profit figure *after* these three deductions (interest, taxation and minority interests) is that we are comparing the return earned for shareholders with what the shareholders have invested: the "return" should therefore not include the three above-mentioned items, which represent the return to lenders, to the Government and to minority shareholders in subsidiaries.

The numerator will then show the *normal or maintainable* profit, which will be related to shareholders' funds. Alternatively we can add/deduct the extra-ordinary gains/losses accruing in the year, thereby arriving at the *total* profit for the year as defined by SSAP 6[1]. These two alternatives for the numerator are then

---

[1]   ASC: Statement of Standard Accounting Practice No 6 Extraordinary items and prior year adjustments, April 1974 with a new part 5 added June 1978.

available to the ratio user: he should use the normal or maintainable profit figure if he is interested in the normal trading return on capital, but he should use the total profit figure if he wishes to calculate the total overall result of the company's activities in the year.

The denominator of the ratio should be the shareholders' funds (capital and reserves, excluding minority interests) at the start of the year. Alternatively, where shareholders' funds have changed materially during the year, the weighted average shareholders' funds figure should be used. This recommendation is based on the need to compare the profit with the capital invested during the period which earned the profit. The principle at stake can be clarified by considering a company which made a large rights issue in the middle of its accounting year. The directors of the company had only six months in which to earn a return on the extra capital and it would be unfair to judge their skills by comparing the year's profit either with the opening figure or with the year-end figure for shareholders' funds. The weighted average figure will produce a ratio which is fair both to the directors and to the providers of the capital. The ratio, as defined above, measures the return on *all* shareholders' capital. If preference dividends are excluded from the numerator and preference capital from the denominator, the ratio measures the return on *ordinary* shareholders' capital.

The adoption of current cost accounting (CCA) has a significant effect on the return on capital. Indeed SSAP 16[2] claims that one of its basic objectives is to provide more useful ratios of return on investment than are available from historical cost accounts, although the SSAP recognises that in some situations CCA may be impracticable or, exceptionally, misleading. The CCA version of return on capital will be calculated by dividing the net current cost profit available for shareholders by the opening (or weighted average) figure for shareholders' funds in current cost terms. This produces a measure of the return earned in real terms, after the operating capacity of the business has been preserved, rather than an inflation-distorted return figure which would only measure the return after the historical capital (eroded by inflation) has been "maintained" in money terms. The inferiority of the ratio based on historical costs arises because it is doubly distorted: the numerator, profit, is generally overstated and the denominator, shareholders' funds, is likely to be understated, so that the ratio is often drastically affected by the measurement convention adopted. For example, Brooke Bond Liebig earned a return of 9% on shareholders' funds on an historical cost basis but only 0.6% on a current cost basis in the year to 30 June 1980. The explanation of the difference between the two figures is that Brooke Bond shareholders could, subject to any liquidity constraints, have been paid a dividend of 9% on their invested funds if they had been content to maintain their investment in terms of a

---

[2] ASC: Statement of Standard Accounting Practice No 16 Current Cost accounting, March 1980.

number of pounds sterling, ignoring inflation. However, if the intention is to maintain shareholders' investment in terms of Brooke Bond's operating capacity, the maximum possible dividend would have been 0.6% of invested funds. In Brooke Bond's case the "maintenance of operating capacity" would mean that the company, faced with various price rises in its inputs, would require to retain sufficient finance to continue to produce a given physical output from its plantations and ranches and also sufficient finance to maintain a constant physical throughput in its packing and distribution activities with tea, coffee, meat and other food products. Under CCA, Brooke Bond would strike a profit figure after setting aside sufficient to finance stocks and debtors at a higher money figure (due to price rises in tea, meat and so on) and to depreciate plant and machinery at its inflated replacement price.

Not all companies are as drastically affected by the change to CCA as Brooke Bond is. In the year to 29 March 1980 British Home Stores earned a return of 23% (historical cost) which became 16% on the current cost basis. These figures of return rates, especially those for Brooke Bond, show that the current cost adjustments are not trivial or merely of academic interest. It is essential that users of the ratio of return on capital should use the current cost information where available, and should press for its disclosure, where it is not yet available, to supplement the historical cost information.

After the return on capital has been calculated, the ratio is compared with the company's own past performance, and trends are noted. It is compared also with the ratios of other companies in the same industry. If the ratios of the company under scrutiny and of its competitors are falling, we are probably looking at a declining industry or at an industry temporarily suffering in a recession. If a company's return on capital is falling behind that of its competitors, the cause may be inefficient investment, under-pricing of products, a poor product range, uneconomic stock-holding practices or a host of other problems. Each of these possibilities can be investigated by referring to the relevant ratios. For example, a suspicion that a relatively poor return on capital is due to poor tax planning will tend to be confirmed if the company's pre-tax return is comparable with that of its competitors whilst its post-tax return is poor.

The discussion of return on capital has so far been limited to the return earned on *shareholders'* funds. Where substantial finance has been raised from sources other than the shareholders, it will often be useful to measure the return on *all* funds invested. For example, suppose two companies, A and B, both operate in the same industry but A relies solely on shareholder finance whilst B borrows a substantial proportion of the necessary finance. It could be that B shows a much higher return on shareholders' funds than A. However, a comparison of the returns on *total* capital invested by each company might reveal no significant difference. We would then conclude that the directors of B were better managers than those of A, but that the superiority lay not in operating activity but in the judicious use of gearing.*

To calculate the return on total funds invested, the total return (*ie*, current cost operating profit, which is arrived at before interest is deducted) is divided by total gross assets (fixed assets plus current assets, all stated at appropriate current values). The resultant ratio could then be described as the percentage earned on all assets, disregarding the method of financing them.

Whilst the return on capital ratio will be of particular interest to investors in a company, the next ratio to be discussed can be approached from the viewpoint of a customer of the company.

Profit to sales

A shopper might visit two adjacent shops, buying cigarettes from one and some jewellery from the other. He will know that the tobacconist's profit on the cigarette sale represents a lower proportion of the sales price than does the jeweller's profit. In taking this view the shopper is implicitly considering the gross profit to sales ratio. The following discussion therefore starts with that ratio before moving on to the operating profit to sales ratio.

The gross profit to sales ratio is constructed by dividing gross profit (*ie*, sales less the actual cost of goods sold) by sales. The ratio will naturally vary with the nature of the trade carried on. In the case of retailers, who, by definition, do not alter the nature of the stock dealt in, gross profit presents no great theoretical problems. For the retailer the gross profit ratio simply measures how much of each pound of sales revenue is available in the form of gross profit to cover operating expenses, taxes and profit. The retailer of cigarettes mentioned above would typically show a gross profit ratio of about 10%, whilst for the jeweller 50% would be more normal. The Inland Revenue and the Customs and Excise authorities are both known to show considerable interest in gross profit ratios. They have tables disclosing the ratios which are normal in each trade and they use these to judge the reliability of the accounts of individual taxpayers. In general a low gross profit ratio is normal where stock turnover is rapid and the goods involve few storage problems and no complicated delivery system. Conversely the ratio has to be high if the trade involves slow-moving stock, costly storage, free delivery or other features which involve heavy costs.

Business policy decisions will affect the ratio: for example one jeweller might decide to operate his business in a way which offered great individual attention to customers by well-trained staff, whilst another decided to operate, so far as was

---

* Gearing ratios are discussed in the later section on ratios which measure liquidity, solvency and financial structure.

practicable, rather like a supermarket with little advice available to customers, less impressive premises and a lower grade of staff. The former jeweller would have to set his prices higher than the latter, in order to cover his greater overheads – in short he would have to price for a higher gross profit to sales ratio, if his return on capital was to be equal to that of his competitor.

The ratio will also be affected by management policy regarding the volume of stock held and the period for which it is held. A business which has a comprehensive stock range and can offer customers immediate delivery of any item ordered, will have to set prices at a level which leads to a relatively high gross profit ratio. Should this policy be changed to one of holding only a limited range of fast-moving goods, the consequent fall in stockholding costs would enable price cuts which lowered the gross profit ratio whilst maintaining return on capital.

The use of the gross profit ratio is not, of course, restricted to retail businesses. It can be used for all businesses which supply goods and for some businesses which supply services.

Once the gross profit ratio has been calculated, it is compared with the company's ratio in earlier years and with the ratio of competitors. Variations in the ratio may reveal poor buying decisions, underpricing of sales or the more general effects of increasing competition in the company's trade. The ratio will also reflect the effect of business policy decisions of the sort described above. The ratio can be readily recalculated on a current cost basis by using as numerator the current cost gross profit, which equals the historical gross profit as amended by the cost of sales adjustment. With inflation this will usually be a debit to profit, thereby reducing the gross profit ratio. (It will, however, be a credit to profit where prices of purchases are falling, for example in electronics, where the cost reductions due to technical innovations have tended to outweigh the effect of inflation on the raw material cost.)

The two sets of gross profit ratios will guide ratio users towards identifying the predominant factors at work. For example, if the company under scrutiny shows a constant historical cost gross profit ratio over the years but a falling current cost gross profit ratio, underpricing will be suspected. If the current cost gross profit ratio of competitors is constant over time this will tend to confirm this suspicion. It could mean that competitors are steadily passing on cost increases to their customers, whilst the company under scrutiny is failing to react rapidly enough. Of course, it could be that the management of the company has deliberately chosen to set prices below those of competitors, perhaps providing a lower level of service (such as delivery and after sales service) and thereby building up their market share. The success of such a policy will show up in sales growth which exceeds that of competitors, in lower overheads than competitors and, eventually, in a superior return on capital, even though the gross profit to sales ratio is lower than that of competitors.

The ratio user will naturally only be able to calculate the gross profit ratio if

5

the accounts from which he is working disclose gross profit as well as turnover. The 1967 Companies Act required that turnover be disclosed in published accounts, but the disclosure of gross profit was rare until the 1981 Act was implemented. This Act permits the company to choose whether to disclose expenses classified by function (*eg*, cost of sales, distribution costs, administrative expenses) or to disclose expenses classified by type (*eg*, raw materials and consumables, staff costs, depreciation). If disclosure by function is chosen, the gross profit is clearly revealed in the profit and loss account and the ratio user has no problem. However, if disclosure by type is chosen, it will depend on the nature of the business whether gross profit can be deduced from the disclosures available. In this case gross profit can be approximated by deducting raw materials and consumables from turnover, but this approximation will be very inaccurate if stocks have changed substantially. (It is true that "change in stocks of finished goods and in work-in-progress" will be disclosed, but it cannot be assumed that this figure contains only raw material costs. The stock valuation could include substantial production overheads, for example.)

In cases where the gross profit figure is not available in the published accounts, ratio users may be able to obtain copies of the company's internal accounts, thereby enabling them to use this ratio: bank lending officers are an example here. When ratio users do not have access to the gross profit figure they are thrown back on the operating profit to sales ratio.

In calculating the operating profit to sales ratio the numerator is amended by deducting all operating expenses which appear in the profit and loss account. The current cost version of this ratio will therefore be affected not merely by the cost of sales adjustment but also by the adjustments to depreciation and monetary working capital. By using operating profit (rather than the net post-tax profit) in the numerator the ratio user will not be affected by the gearing policy of the company. This is because the gearing, whether high or low, only affects the profit after interest and not the operating profit which is struck before interest is deducted. For many companies the current cost adjustments result in a loss. This makes the profit ratio negative. In these circumstances calculating the ratio drives home the message of current cost accounting. For example, if the ratio is minus 2%, this means that shareholders are incurring a loss of £2 for each £100 worth of sales. Another way of describing this would be to say that for each £100 of sales, the real wealth of the shareholders, in terms of the operating capacity which they indirectly "own" through the company, is being dissipated by £2. The shareholders are steadily becoming poorer because they are selling for £100 a product which costs the company £102. The shareholders could be said to be subsidising customers by £2 per £100 of sales.

The interpretation of the profit to sales ratio is greatly helped by calculating a number of additional ratios dealing with expenses. The trend of the selling expenses to sales ratio, and a comparison with competitors, will provide some information on the company's policy regarding its sales force. For instance, a policy of raising sales by means of an active, well-equipped and well-rewarded team of salesmen will produce a high ratio of selling costs to sales. An alternative policy would be to concentrate on advertising and to seek to raise sales through a large advertising campaign backed up by a smaller sales team whose function is chiefly to take orders rather than actively to persuade potential customers to buy. The ratios of selling costs to sales and of marketing costs to sales will disclose this type of policy difference between competing companies, and will indicate any change of policy in a given company. The source of expertise on these various additional ratios is the Centre for Interfirm Comparison.* The Centre has considerable experience at calculating and interpreting comparable ratios for groups of similar companies and so is able to throw much light on the underlying causes for variations in the net profit ratio.

The two measures of profitability and performance which have been discussed have combined profit and capital invested, and profit and sales. This leads on to a further ratio which relates sales to capital invested.

Sales to Capital

This ratio describes the operating characteristics of the company and the industry in which it operates. Industries vary greatly in the amount of capital required to generate a given turnover, and these differences are revealed by dividing sales revenue by capital employed.

In constructing the ratio a choice exists between using either total capital or merely the capital provided by shareholders (*ie*, issued share capital plus reserves). The total capital figure is more appropriate for obtaining a broad view of the nature of a trade. By using the total capital as denominator the turnover is regarded as having been generated by all assets, fixed and current. The alternative of using the shareholders' funds as the denominator will be more appropriate if the ratio user is principally concerned with the shareholders' welfare. For example, an investor who is thinking of purchasing 100% of the equity of a company in a given trade will do well to consider the ratio of sales to the capital invested by shareholders, and to compare this ratio amongst the various companies on his list for possible purchase. This will firstly give him some idea of the characteristics of the trade he is about to enter, and secondly draw to his attention any significant differences between the companies available. These differences could be due to differing efficiency or differing management policies.

---

* The Centre was established in 1959 by the British Institute of Management and the British Productivity Council. The Centre's address is 8 West Stockwell Street, Colchester, Essex, CO1 1HN.

A further choice faces the ratio user in constructing this ratio: the capital employed figure (whether total capital or shareholders' funds) can be measured either on a historical cost or a current cost basis. The current cost figure, when available, will normally be the more useful, for the ratio will then compare sales, measured in current pounds, with the current cost accounting value of assets, also measured in current pounds. If the fixed assets have been purchased several years before the balance sheet date, the current cost capital figure will generally be much higher than the historical cost figure (due to inflation over the years the assets had been held) and therefore the current cost sales to capital ratio will be lower than the historical cost version. An exception to this would be found in a company holding assets whose prices are not subject to inflation, an example being a television rental company, which would be affected by falling replacement costs for its fixed assets, such as video recorders.

Subject, of course, to the inevitable characteristics of the trade, a high figure for sales to capital is preferable to a low one. Managers should seek to generate a large turnover (provided, of course, the sales are profitable) from the given capital, or, conversely, to minimise the investment required in order to generate the given turnover.

Many industries report a ratio of sales to (historical cost) total capital of around 2, but a consideration of extreme cases helps to clarify what influences the ratio. The Ladbroke Group's sales to capital ratio was over 15 in 1969 but had decreased to just over 2 by the end of 1980. In 1969 the Group ran a chain of betting shops. The "sales" figure in the gambling industry is the total of gross bets placed, and it is obvious that a high sales figure can be generated from a given capital because the same amounts of cash reappear often in sales. The customer who places a £5 bet might expect, on average, to receive back say £4.50, assuming he has no great talent at judging horseflesh. The next day he may bet another £5 and, from the betting shop's point of view, yesterday's payout of customers' winnings often becomes tomorrow's sales. The fall in Ladbroke's ratio over the eleven-year period was due to diversification. The Group's activities now involve hotels, property development, holidays, restaurants, retailing, taverns and bingo clubs as well as their traditional betting shops. The hotel trade inevitably has a low sales to capital ratio. A hotel may involve building costs of £15,000 per bedroom and the average bedroom, if charged out at £20 per night for, say, 300 nights, will produce only £6,000 per annum: a sales to capital ratio of under one-half. The hotel as a whole will report a higher sales to capital ratio because the food and beverage part of the trade will raise the ratio. For example, the ratio for Trusthouse Forte was 1.3 in 1980.

A perusal of the accounts of a selection of companies which are all in the same trade will give rise to the idea of a norm for the sales to capital ratio in that trade. Deviations from the norm can then be investigated. These deviations may be due to efficiency variations. For example, an unusually low ratio could indicate

8

underutilisation of capacity. On the other hand, the deviations could be due to deliberate management decisions. An obvious example would be the decision as to whether to rent or buy premises, because purchased premises would augment capital invested and so lower the ratio. The ratio will also be affected by management's reaction to the prices of different factors of production: where labour is cheap, management will tend to choose labour intensive production methods. Where labour is costly, capital intensive production will be chosen. One would, therefore, expect the sales to capital ratio in a given industry to be higher in New Delhi than in New York.

It is often helpful to combine the reporting of this ratio with the two previous ones, thus:

$$(1)\ \frac{\text{profit}}{\text{capital}} = (2)\ \frac{\text{profit}}{\text{sales}} \times (3)\ \frac{\text{sales}}{\text{capital}}$$

The purpose of the above simple equation is that it brings out the relationship between the ratios. For example, the equation makes it clear that a company with an unusually low ratio of turnover to capital will require an unusually large sales margin in order to achieve a given ratio of return on capital. Also the equation guides the ratio user as to the right questions to ask. If (1) in the equation is deteriorating over time relative to competitors, we can start to analyse why from the right-hand side. If (3) is steady but (2) is falling, the cause could be under-pricing of output, or perhaps inefficiency and rising costs incurred at a constant volume of business. If (2) is steady but (3) is falling, this could be due to under-utilisation of capacity or surplus, idle assets such as excessive stock levels; or the cause could be market changes, such as increased competition or commitment to an obsolete product. A company might, as a matter of policy, choose to trade in a deterioration in ratios (2) or (3) for an improvement in the other ratio. For example, it might be decided to cut prices (reducing ratio (2)) in the hope that sales would increase substantially (raising ratio (3)). This policy could be judged successful if ratio (1) showed an improvement after the policy change. Another illustration on these lines is provided by a company which adopts a policy of substituting capital for labour wherever possible, for example by investing heavily in computers and word processors to replace clerks. This will cause (3) to deteriorate, but the hope will be that the rise in (2) will more than compensate for this. (Ratio (2) will rise if the extra depreciation and interest on the new fixed assets are less than the savings in labour costs, so that profit to sales will improve.)

The three ratios which have so far been discussed bring out the relationships between profit, capital and sales. The next ratio to be investigated analyses the company's sales by reporting the extent to which the company itself has created the value of output.

Value added to sales

The numerator of this ratio, value added, is a performance measure, as is profit. The difference between the two performance measures is that profit measures performance from the narrow viewpoint of shareholders' welfare alone, whilst value added offers a broader concept of performance. Value added measures the wealth created by the company for all capital providers and employees and for the Government. It therefore reports the contribution which the company has made to the financial welfare of all participators or stakeholders in the company.

The reward earned by this team of participators is measured by taking sales, which is the value of all output, and deducting all expenses which relate to goods or services purchased from other companies. Having thus deducted that part of the sales value which represents the value added by other companies (*ie*, by suppliers), we arrive at the figure for the value added by the company itself, which measures the wealth created in the year by the co-operative efforts of capital providers, employees and management. This figure for value added represents the amount which became available in the year for various purposes, including rewarding the team of participators: the distribution includes the pay of employees of all classes (including directors and managers), the taxes paid to government, which has provided the economic and legal infrastructure, and the interest and dividends paid to capital providers, with the balance (if any) being retained to finance the expansion, development and diversification of the company.

The value added is then divided by sales, thereby revealing the proportion of sales revenue which has been created by the efforts of participators in the company as opposed to being created by the company's suppliers. The ratio is low where the company has itself done little to the output, for example where a retailer has merely provided a distribution service but not altered the nature of the goods. Conversely the ratio is high (perhaps approaching its upper limit, which is unity) where the company has itself generated most of the value of its output using its own workforce and fixed assets.

Inter-company comparisons of the ratio of value added to sales provide a useful description of the company studied and its policies, rather than an assessment of it. This ratio is not like return on capital – where a high value is desirable, or like gearing – where a low value is thought safe.

The ratio of value added to sales indicates the extent to which a company's trading activities are vertically or horizontally integrated. Vertical integration refers to the trading entity which results when a company buys up its suppliers (and its suppliers' suppliers) so that the one company controls the entire production chain, from raw material acquisition through to the sale to the eventual consumer. The case of a multinational oil company provides an example, because the company extracts crude oil, carries it in its own fleet of marine tankers, refines the

10

oil and participates in retailing the final products. Such a company will show a relatively high ratio of value added to sales, since there are relatively low purchases from the few outside suppliers who have not been absorbed by the multinational.

Horizontal integration, on the other hand, arises when a company performs just one process in the sequence of processes between raw material and final product, and it expands by opening new branches (or by buying out competitors) which perform the same process. An example of this is the multiple chain store company. Such a company has decided to expand by carrying out the same single activity (retail distribution) in many geographical locations rather than to expand by acquiring its suppliers. A horizontally integrated company naturally has relatively high purchases from outside suppliers and hence a relatively low value added to sales ratio.

The current cost version of value added is more useful, both generally and in this ratio, than the historical cost version. This is because it measures the value which has been added by *productive* efforts. It does not blur the facts by stirring in the "value" added to output by price changes during the productive period.

Putting this in practical terms: consider a company which buys raw materials in January for £10,000 and works on them throughout the year. The output is sold for £25,000 in December, by which time the current cost of replacing the raw materials has risen to £12,000. In these circumstances the historical value added in the year, ignoring all complications over depreciation and so on but concentrating on the price variation, will be £15,000, being £25,000 sales less the historical cost of materials at £10,000. The current cost value added will be £13,000, being £25,000 sales less the current cost of materials (£12,000). If the value added figure is measured in order to indicate the productive achievements of the company, it is clearly misleading to include, without explanation, the £2,000 price uplift in the value added figure. It is better to remove from value added this £2,000 holding gain. This gain may be due to general inflation, as will be the case if virtually all commodities, goods and services have risen in price by a similar percentage over the same period. Alternatively the gain may be due to good management. This will apply if the company's buyers have correctly predicted that this category of raw materials will rise in price during the year at a rate faster than the rate of general inflation. In this case, by purchasing in advance of the price rise, management will have made a gain of a non-recurrent nature.

Having compared value added with sales, the next step is to monitor how value added is shared amongst the participators in the company. As the lion's share of value added usually goes to the workforce, the ratio showing that proportion is of particular interest.

Value added to payroll costs

This ratio measures labour productivity. It is generally agreed that economic growth and increases in living standards are conditional on productivity increases. The ratio of value added to payroll costs, by providing a measure of labour productivity, enables the ratio user to make inter-company comparisons of productivity, and to monitor any productivity trends within a business. This monitoring function helps the ratio user to assess the soundness of management strategies and to identify businesses with real prospects of survival and growth.

The ratio is simply constructed. Current cost value added is divided by the year's gross payroll charge, the latter including employers' social security and pension fund contributions. Some accountants prefer to include the cost of employees' fringe benefits under payroll costs, but these benefits are difficult to measure precisely in practice. There is little point in spending time deciding whether awkward borderline items like car park maintenance or an industrial health service are a fringe benefit or a general expense. These borderline items should be omitted from payroll costs as they are seldom material and their inclusion gives scope for time-wasting arguments between management and employees' representatives. Rather than argue over trivial points of definition, both parties should participate in efforts to improve the ratio.

The ratio is, in practice, often inverted so that it then measures the proportion of value added which has gone on wages, pensions and social security contributions. This inversion may be rather unwise as it could lead to a misunderstanding by employees, who might wrongly infer that wage cuts are planned. The real intention of management will be to achieve a higher value added per pound of wages cost, and this goal is quite compatible with increased wages.

One company which has published its ratio of wages costs to value added is Allied Breweries. The trend in labour productivity is as follows:

	1974/75	75/76	76/77	78/79	79/80	80/81
Wages costs to value added	57.2%	60.1%	59.5%	65.4%	68.5%	69.2%

(Value added is measured on a historical cost basis in arriving at the above ratios. A worse picture would be painted of labour productivity if the figures for current cost value added were used.)

This sequence of ratios shows clearly the trend in labour productivity, which is not reassuring to shareholders in Allied: a steadily increasing share of the value which has been added by the joint efforts of workers and capital providers is going in wages to the workforce. Less is therefore left available for reinvestment.

Having used the ratio of payroll costs to value added as a measure of labour productivity, attention can now be turned from the workforce back to the capital providers and to shareholders in particular. The final ratio discussed in this section offers a measure of performance per share.

Earnings per share (EPS)

Ratio users often need to assess the value of a company's shares. In so doing it is natural to consider the earnings, or post-tax profits, per share. The EPS is, to a large extent, the source of the share's value because the earnings will be either paid out as dividend to the holder of the share or will be retained, thereby enhancing the company's assets and generating a capital gain on the share.

The idea of dividing earnings by the number of shares seems straightforward, but in practice the ratio can conceal a number of subtleties. To start with, the number of shares (the denominator of the ratio) may have changed in the past year or may be liable to change in the future. A rights or bonus issue in the past year will render the ratio non-comparable with the EPS figure for earlier years. Changes in the future may arise from the exercise of options or of warrant rights. In these circumstances the diluted EPS figure must be calculated as well as the crude or undiluted EPS.

SSAP 3[3] deals with these problems by standardising the adjustments to the number of shares in issue. This SSAP was issued in 1972 and amended in 1974 when the imputation system of corporation tax was adopted. This system involves a different level of tax on profit depending on whether the profit is distributed or retained. The treatment of corporation tax in the numerator of the EPS ratio is adequately explained in SSAP 3 when read alongside SSAP 8[4], which standardises the treatment of corporation tax in annual accounts.

The numerator of the EPS ratio must be handled with some care if comparability is to be achieved. The post-tax profit available for *equity* shareholders must be used: any dividend entitlement of preference shareholders should be omitted from the numerator because the preference shares are omitted from the denominator.

The post-tax profit which is used as numerator will be affected by the company's provisions (if any) for deferred tax. These provisions should be based on SSAP 15[5], which broadly speaking requires that deferred taxation be provided for, except that going concerns need not make provisions if no tax liability is likely to arise from reversal of timing differences for at least three years ahead. The formation of opinions as to the likelihood of reversal within three years is a rather subjective matter. The likelihood will depend on policies for the replacement and expansion of plant and buildings over the next three-year period, which

---

[3] ASC: Statement of Standard Accounting Practice No 3 Earnings per share, revised August 1974.

[4] ASC: Statement of Standard Accounting Practice No 8 The treatment of taxation under the imputation system in the accounts of companies, August 1974, with new part added December 1977.

[5] ASC: Statement of Standard Accounting Practice No 15 Accounting for deferred taxation, October 1978.

will inevitably be tentative and conditional in many businesses. To avoid being misled by differences between companies in deferred taxation policies, the ratio user should make a point of reading the notes to the accounts before comparing the EPS figures of different companies.

Another complication is that SSAP 3 requires that post-tax profit *before* extraordinary items be used as the numerator of EPS. This is sensible because the extraordinary items are the infrequent and unusual gains and losses which would blur the predictive value of a year-by-year series for EPS. However, the relative importance of extraordinary items should be kept in mind when assessing an EPS ratio.

The EPS figure must be disclosed in current cost terms by listed companies, and SSAP 16 requires the numerator of current cost EPS to be the current cost profit attributable to equity shareholders before extraordinary items. It is important to use the attributable profit rather than the operating profit as numerator because then the amount available for equity holders is divided by the number of equity claims.

To illustrate some of the points made above, the EPS for £1 ordinary shares in Bowater were:

	1980	1979
Historical cost EPS	18.8 pence	33.1 pence
Current cost EPS	3.8 pence	20.6 pence

Perusal of the notes to Bowater's accounts reveals that the Group appears to be using the exception clause of SSAP 15 and not providing for deferred tax and that the potential dilution due to the Group's convertible loan stock is negligible. However, the notes also reveal material extraordinary redundancy costs in 1980: had EPS been measured using post-tax profit *after* these extraordinary items, historical EPS would have been about 2 pence in 1980 and current cost EPS would have been a negative 5 pence (*ie*, 5 pence loss per share). The magnitude of these changes in the EPS figures underlines the need to read the notes to the accounts.

14

2 Ratios Measuring Liquidity, Solvency and Financial Structure

Every company will be expected to achieve certain objectives, and these objectives will change over the years with social attitudes and conditions. The social objectives set for a company may at different times include such diverse aims as job creation, customer satisfaction and contributing to the defence of the nation (as by producing food or weapons in wartime). For each company and social objective there will be some criterion by which success may be judged. As this monograph is restricted to the uses of ratios derived from annual accounts, the wider social objectives of a company have to be set aside and attention concentrated on the profitability and survival of the concern.

The main ratios used to assess profitability have been reviewed, but the ability to earn profits does not necessarily guarantee survival. A company must also be able to meet its liabilities as they become due; failure to do so will entail a risk of bankruptcy or liquidation.

Those who lend to the company will naturally be concerned as to its liquidity and solvency. These two terms are not identical in meaning. Liquidity refers to assets and is applicable when an asset can quickly and easily be converted to cash. Solvency on the other hand refers to the balance, or lack of it, between liabilities due for early settlement and the quantity and liquidity of the assets available to meet these liabilities. Absolute solvency, which is measured at a particular date, means that a company's entire assets, if realised, would be sufficient to meet all its liabilities. Practical solvency implies the existence, in a going concern, of a sufficient inflow of cash to meet all its short-term liabilities as they become due in the ordinary course of business.

Lenders will also take an interest in the company's financial structure. This last term describes the proportions which exist between the sources from which the company has financed its assets: finance will have come partly from shareholders and partly from long and short-term lenders. An imprudent financial structure would suggest that the company may have difficulty meeting its payments and obligations and be unable to finance its operations in the medium- or long-term future. An example of such a structure would be one in which an excessively high proportion of finance has been raised in the form of short-term borrowing. The ratios which measure liquidity or solvency are therefore more concerned with the short-term future, whilst those which measure financial structure are designed more for longer-term assessments. The discussion of the relevant ratios starts with those which have a shorter time horizon.

Current ratio (or working capital ratio)

The widely used current ratio measures the short-term liquidity position of the company and enables the user to assess the adequacy of working capital and risk of insolvency. The ratio is constructed by dividing current assets by current liabilities. Since current assets are principally stock, debtors and cash, and current liabilities are those due for payment within the year following the balance sheet date, it can be seen that this ratio measures the proportion which liquid assets (*ie*, cash plus assets due to be converted into cash in the near future) bear to short-term commitments. The former should normally exceed the latter by a reasonable margin.

It is often said that this ratio should produce a figure of at least two for safety. That rule of thumb can be very misleading, because much depends on the nature of the trade and on management's policy regarding working capital. The policy on stockholding might be to carry an extensive range or merely to carry fast-moving lines. Production policy might be to produce only for firm orders or to produce steadily for stock; and extended credit might be offered to attract customers or sales might be made only for cash. Each of these policy decisions would affect the size and composition of current assets and would affect the current ratio.

Many companies have operated successfully for years with a current ratio much lower than two. Recent current ratios, extracted from accounts published for accounting years ending in 1980, include 1.0 (Godfrey Davis), 1.2 (Unigate), 1.5 (Allied Breweries), 1.8 (Chloride), 2.1 (Racal) and 2.5 (Great Universal Stores). (The last-mentioned company has a relatively high ratio because half its current assets are in the form of future hire-purchase instalments receivable, which naturally take considerable time to collect and are not immediately available, so that a higher current ratio is prudent). The foregoing list of ratios shows that the "two-to-one" rule of thumb is by no means universally relevant.

Another flaw in the "two-to-one" rule is that a ratio of two does not guarantee solvency. Consider, for example, a distillery with a current ratio of 3. If this ratio is produced by current assets of £3 million which are almost all in the form of slow-to-mature stocks, but the current liabilities of £1 million represent creditors and tax liabilities due for payment in the succeeding few months, then early and serious liquidity problems can be expected, despite the apparently satisfactory current ratio.

The warning was given above that the two-to-one guideline for the current ratio should not be applied too rigidly. It remains true, however, that a low current ratio is often an indication of the serious problem of overtrading. A current ratio which declines over the years, or one which is substantially lower than that of comparable companies, should be investigated; it may be indicating a danger of forced liquidation and possible losses for creditors.

If overtrading is diagnosed then, provided the company is basically profitable, the cure is a sizeable increase in long-term funds invested. The further investment has to be long term since an increase in short-term finance will, by definition, require early repayment and will therefore merely continue the pattern of trading at a level which is too ambitious for the limited capital invested. Management would be spending excessive time on handling constant short-term problems to the detriment of the long-term future of the concern. The additional long-term finance should be raised from shareholders, perhaps by a rights issue, or from long-term loans. The decision between these alternatives would largely depend on the gearing ratio, which is discussed later in this section.

An over-high current ratio suggests a different problem – that of excessive levels of current assets. If the management of the company has not given sufficient attention to current assets, it may be that the company has slipped into the habit of holding excessive stocks or cash balances or of failing to collect its debts promptly. In the case of stocks there is the natural desire of production management to have raw materials constantly available so that production is never held up. It could be that the danger of running out of raw materials has been overcompensated for and the practice has grown up of re-ordering raw materials excessively early, so that the stores are almost always full. Similarly, in the case of debtors, the company may be sending out statements to customers at two-monthly intervals when it could achieve early receipts by doing this monthly.

These faults are merely suggested, not proved, by a high current ratio. The explanation of the high ratio could be more favourable to management. It could be that the deliberate policy of the business is to hold higher stock levels than those of competitors – thereby enabling a better service to customers by offering a wider choice range and greater likelihood of early delivery from stock. Offering extended payment periods to customers could also be a sensible policy for management to pursue in order to increase sales, though the price charged to customers should reflect this additional facility.

The numerical value of the current ratio directs the ratio user towards asking the right questions, but additional information is needed to answer these questions. For example, a high current ratio, caused by higher stock levels than normal, could, as has been seen above, be due to deliberate policy or to inertia in stock management (ie, inefficient use of capital). The gross profit to sales ratio would help distinguish between the two, since the policy of holding large stocks to offer superior service to customers should be rewarded by higher sales prices.

17

It may be objected that slackness in debtor control will not affect the current ratio because both debtors and cash are included in the numerator. Therefore, it may be argued, even if the business improves its practices and achieves more rapid collection from debtors, the fall in the debtors figure will be balanced by a rise in the cash figure and so the current ratio will not fall. This objection has little merit, however, because the rise in the cash figure (resulting from more rapid debtor collection) should obviously not be held permanently in cash. Rather than being held in the form of a non-earning asset, the cash should be used for some purpose, depending on the company's needs. Perhaps trade creditors could be paid earlier, thus earning discounts, or loans could be repaid or profitable fixed assets could be acquired. Each of these uses for the cash would have some effect on the current ratio.

The company's stocks appear, of course, in the numerator of the current ratio and their inclusion is one of the weak points of the ratio. This is because the value at which the stocks are shown will usually be more subjective than the values of the other current assets. What is more, the stock value will often be drastically reduced if the company does later go into liquidation with the stock being sold other than in the ordinary course of business.

Two rather technical points must also be kept in mind regarding stocks in cases where there is doubt as to whether the company is a going concern. First, it could be that the company does not have unfettered ownership of the stocks if it has purchased them subject to reservation of title by the seller (*ie*, a Romalpa-type[1] clause in the acquisition contract). Second, it may be that one of the creditors holds a floating charge over the stock. If either of these applies, then the ratio can be misleading since the stock is not potentially available to the general creditors. The remedy is to re-calculate the ratio, omitting the stock affected from the numerator and omitting the related liability from the denominator.

A further consideration regarding the effect of stock on the current ratio is that, where possible, the ratio should be calculated from the current cost balance sheet rather than from the historical cost balance sheet. The difference will arise because the current cost version of the current ratio will incorporate the stocks at their current value. For businesses which turn over stocks rapidly, such as food retailers, the difference between the two current ratios will always be negligible. Where, however, stock is very slow moving, and replacement costs have risen since the stock was acquired, the current cost version of the ratio will be rather higher and will give a more accurate view of the current asset value which is available to meet current liabilities.

The current ratio should be evaluated bearing in mind the notes to the accounts. The notes might disclose substantial contingent liabilities or

[1] Institute of Chartered Accountants of Scotland (in association with other professional bodies), "Accounting for goods sold subject to reservation of title", July 1976.

commitments already contracted for future capital expenditure. These are relevant when considering the current position and in an extreme case could cast doubt on the liquidity of the concern even though the current ratio is apparently satisfactory. Information may also be available on the extension or reduction of overdraft facilities available over the few months following the balance sheet date, and this information might change the view taken as to the adequacy of short-term liquid assets.

In summary, the current ratio is an invaluable coarse screening device in judging the adequacy of working capital and practical (but not absolute) solvency, but it should be used carefully. The ratio user should not rigidly judge the current ratios he calculates according to the two-to-one rule, because it has been seen that a current ratio of two would in some cases not ensure solvency and in others would indicate inefficiently high holdings of current assets. Particular consideration should be given to the characteristics of the trade, the policies adopted by management, the trend in the ratio, the comparison with those of competitors and any supplementary information available which affects current assets or current liabilities. The final judgment on practical solvency and on the adequacy of working capital should not be made merely on the current ratio but should incorporate the other relevant ratios and the cash flow information provided in the statement of source and application of funds.

Liquid asset ratio (or quick asset ratio or acid test*)

We have seen that the inclusion of stock in the numerator of the current ratio leads to a number of reservations as to the usefulness of that ratio. The liquid ratio seeks to get around this problem by excluding stock from the numerator. The ratio is therefore current assets less stock (which is the same as debtors plus cash, plus other liquid assets such as short-term investments) divided by current liabilities. It is often useful to amend this by excluding overdrafts from the denominator where they are of a semi-permanent nature. In some trades overdrafts fluctuate cyclically over the year as stocks are built up and run down in the seasonal trading pattern. In these cases, including such overdrafts in the denominator will produce large and potentially misleading fluctuations in the liquid ratio, which will then include the overdraft but exclude the stocks thereby financed. The exclusion of these over-drafts from the ratio produces a figure more relevant to the needs of short-term creditors (other than the bank), especially since in these trades the overdraft is often secured by a floating charge over the stock.

The resultant ratio compares the assets which are already liquid (cash)

---

* The term "acid test" is used by some accountants to refer to the ratio of *cash* to current liabilities rather than as a synonym for the liquid asset ratio).

together with those which should very soon be liquid (debtors) with liabilities due for payment in the immediate future. It is therefore a shorter-term ratio than the current ratio.

The popular rule of thumb here is that the ratio should not be less than unity. This rule is basically sensible in that one does expect immediately available liquid resources to exceed immediate liabilities, but it is too rigid to be applied to all companies. It is, for example, not unusual to find a supermarket with a liquid ratio of around 0.15. This may be quite acceptable because all sales are for cash and, the business having no debtors, all the liquid assets are instantly available cash and this cash is constantly being replenished by rapid stock disposal. Furthermore, the trade creditors know that the stock they have sold to the supermarket will rapidly be re-sold. Industrial companies should, however, have a ratio which is not too far below one. Recent liquid ratios extracted from published accounts include 0.3 (British Home Stores), 0.6 (Allied Breweries) and 0.9 (Chloride Group).

The liquid ratio is not affected, of course, by current cost adjustments. As with the current ratio, the trend in the liquid ratio of the business and the comparison with rivals in the same trade are essential in order to judge the adequacy of liquidity, although the fact that a company's liquid ratio is similar to those of its rivals will not necessarily indicate that the company's liquidity is adequate; the whole trade could be in a dangerous situation. It should be realised that this ratio can be greatly affected by contracts entered into just before the balance sheet date or deliberately postponed until just after that date. For example, a large sale to a credit customer just before the accounting date will lower stocks and raise debtors, thereby improving the ratio. A more serious example is the deliberate postponement of a routine purchase of raw materials from a supplier until just after the accounting date. This will postpone the resulting increase in creditors and thereby avoid making the liquid ratio seem unfavourable on that date. These problems of window dressing are discussed further in the final section of this paper.

Debtors turnover

If the annual turnover of a business is divided by the average debtors figure the resulting ratio reveals the number of times debtors are turned over in a year. If this ratio is inverted the resultant figure represents a fraction of a year, which can then be multiplied by 365 to produce the average number of calendar days which debtors take to pay. (Or it can be multiplied by 250 to arrive at the average number of working days which they take to pay, assuming a five-day week. Both of these average payment delays may, in some trades, conceal substantial seasonal variation in the actual payment delays).

The ratio is therefore a reflection of the combination of trade practice and the effectiveness of the company's credit control. A rapid turnover of debtors, which is the same as a low number of days in the inverted ratio, is desirable but is not feasible in some trades. For example, the merchant who supplies farmers will inevitably have a relatively high debtors balance compared with a merchant who supplies retailers. This is attributable to the traditional trade practice whereby farmers are allowed extended credit because they tend to receive their sales revenue unevenly over the year. Sales receipts will naturally be concentrated in the post-harvest months and it is convenient for the farmer to postpone paying his debts until the harvest has been sold.

An example at the opposite end of the spectrum from the agricultural merchant is the supermarket, where all sales are for cash. In that trade the debtors turnover is not applicable because there are no debtors.

Most industrial companies turn over their debtors somewhere between four and twelve times per annum, ie, the typical payment delay will be somewhere between three months and one month. Where the trade is highly seasonal this ratio can be misleading unless one can obtain month-by-month figures for debtors.

Whilst rapid debtor turnover is desirable, there are naturally limits on achieving this, for one might substantially lower sales if one lost customers through aggressive insistence on early payment. When debtor turnover is slowing down over successive years and is slower than that of competitors, the cause will usually be that management has not paid enough attention to its credit management policy and the control of its implementation. Changes in business policy which affect the debtors figure will also affect the debtors turnover. Management might decide to factor its debts, in effect selling its sales ledger balances to a finance house at a discount, which would include the interest element on the accelerated sales receipts. This policy would cause the reported debtors turnover ratio to rise in terms of times turned over per annum. The introduction of revised contractual arrangements with customers, enabling them to obtain a cash discount for early settlement, would have a similar, though less dramatic, effect.

The current cost adjustments are not relevant to this ratio, because the figures for debtors and for sales are not altered by the change from historical to current costs.

Having seen how debtors turnover is calculated and used, it is natural to apply the same approach to stock.

Stock turnover

Ideally this ratio should be constructed by dividing the cost of sales during the past year by the average stock held. The cost of sales figure has become more widely available due to the disclosure requirements of the 1981 Companies Act, though there are still cases where the figure is not available, for example where the company chooses the alternative format for its profit and loss account. In these cases a compromise solution is to divide sales by the average stock. This compromise is rather unsatisfactory because the numerator of the ratio includes output at selling price whilst the denominator includes output at cost price.

The ratio, once constructed, represents the number of times per annum the stock is turned over. If the ratio is inverted and converted to days, it reveals the average number of days the company's product has been held in stock before being sold. The ratio reflects the characteristics of the industry and the efficiency of management's stock control. The stock of a distillery or of an antique dealer will turn over very slowly, whilst the greengrocer or fishmonger represents the opposite case – for obvious reasons! A typical industrial company will tend to turn over its stock about four times per annum.

Subject to the constraints of the industry, fast stock turnover indicates popular products and an efficient production cycle, though inadequate stock levels may disrupt smooth production runs and may lose orders from customers who will not tolerate delayed delivery. Excessive stocks and slow moving, unpopular product lines will incur high storage and finance costs.

The average stock figure in the denominator of the ratio will be the average of the opening and closing stocks if the ratio is constructed from the published accounts alone. This will not be too misleading unless the company's trade is very seasonal. In seasonal trades the stock will fluctuate greatly over the year and the accounting year-end will usually be chosen in the month when stocks are at their lowest, for example after the January sales for a department store, since this minimises the costs and disruption of stocktaking. In these cases the sales to average stock ratio will falsely imply that the average stock turnover is much faster than the true figure. The ideal solution in seasonal trades is to obtain the month-by-month stock figures and to calculate the true average stock from these, using this true average in place of the crude average derived merely from the (untypical) opening and closing stock figures.

If the stock turnover is getting slower over successive accounting periods, and if it slower than that of competing companies, there are clear signs of danger – suggesting a failure by management to review its stockholding policy. Consideration should be given to policies of abandoning slow-moving products and running down stocks to more balanced levels.

Where the accounts contain sufficient detail to permit it, the ratio user should calculate the stock turnover by different lines of business. As an illustration, the stock turnover of Marks and Spencer appears to be over 16 times per annum from their 1981 accounts (though this is inevitably an overestimate because sales has been used as a proxy for cost of sales in the numerator). This composite figure of 16 is merely a weighted average of the fast stock turnover in the company's food departments and the slower turnover in clothing and household goods.

This point is relatively easy to grasp in the case of a retailer like Marks &

Spencer. It can be extended to the more complex position of an industrial company, the stock figure of which will comprise raw materials, work in progress and finished goods. If the ratio user had access to the detailed management accounts he could calculate the turnover in each category. For example, it could be that management have, as a matter of policy, slowed down raw materials turnover (to provide a buffer stock because incoming supplies are expected to be disrupted by strikes or political instability in supplier countries) but have accelerated the turnover of finished goods (for cash flow reasons).

Having reviewed the ratios which are helpful in judging the short term, the next step is to move to the longer term. This involves abandoning the emphasis on the current assets, which has pervaded the last four ratios, and extending the coverage of the ratios to the financing of the entire asset base of the business.

Gearing ratio (or leverage, proprietary, or debt-to equity ratio)

This family of ratios describes the company's financial structure and measures the long-term risk implied by that structure. They reveal the balance between the two sources of long-term finance: the funds invested by shareholders and those invested by lenders. If long-term debt is divided by long-term debt plus shareholders' funds, the resulting ratio shows the proportion of long-term funds provided by lenders to the business. This would usually be described as the gearing or leverage ratio because high gearing describes a financial structure which is heavy with debt.

The term "gearing" is used by analogy with a mechanical system of gears. Gears have the effect that a given degree of movement in one part of a system (such as a car engine) can have a large or a small effect elsewhere in the system (such as the car's wheels), depending on whether a high or low gear is selected. Where financial gearing is high, a relatively small change in operating profit or in asset values will have a substantial effect on equity earnings or equity values.

To bring this out in another way, suppose D represents the debt or borrowing a company has incurred, E represents shareholders' equity and A represents the assets financed by D and E,

then the equation $E + D = A$ describes the balance sheet.

Gearing is defined as $\dfrac{D}{D + E}$

The extreme case of low gearing would be where $D = 0$; in fact there is no gearing in this case. If this is so, then $E = A$ and a 10% change in asset values (*ie*, in A) will change E by 10%.

Now consider a case of relatively high gearing where $E = D$. This means the company is financed equally by debt and equity. As in the previous case, let it be supposed that A rises by 10%. D will not be affected, because the obligation to repay debts does not rise merely because the borrower's assets have risen in value. The whole of the rise in asset values accrues to E, which therefore rises by 20%. The balance sheet effect of the change is as follows (assuming the initial asset values were 100):

Before				After			
E	50	A	100	E	60	A	110
D	50			D	50		

It can be seen how the 10% rise in A has caused E to rise by 20% and therefore why the term "gearing" is appropriate. North Americans tend to use the word "leverage" rather than gearing, which again represents a suitable mechanical analogy.

It has been seen that gearing, or leverage is $\dfrac{D}{D + E}$. Some users of the ratio prefer to use a variant of this, the proprietary ratio, namely $\dfrac{E}{D + E}$. It is obvious that this ratio measures the shareholders' (or proprietors') contribution to long-term finance and that the gearing and proprietary ratios sum to unity.

A third way of measuring gearing is the debt to equity ratio, which is D/E.

For consistency the following discussion is expressed in terms of the gearing ratio, expressed as a percentage, but the conclusions can readily be re-expressed in terms of the two other variants described.

The basic rule for lenders to the business is that a high gearing ratio is more risky than a low one and is seen as a warning sign. Over-reliance on borrowing, especially in times of high interest rates, can mean that a downturn in operating earnings will threaten the due payment of interest. This threat would be much less if gearing were low, for there would then be a substantial cushion of equity earnings to absorb the fall in earnings before there was any real risk to the interest recipients. High gearing, by implying more risk of the non-payment of interest, also renders receivership or liquidation more likely if business deteriorates. The company with low gearing may therefore be expected to survive temporary setbacks whilst the company with high gearing imposes risks on those from whom it has borrowed. A low gearing ratio is an indication of stability and safety for long-term creditors, since any fall in operating earnings or company asset values would then have to be very substantial before the creditors would be exposed to the risk of non-payment of their interest or capital on the due dates, or of insufficient company assets to repay their loans in the event of a winding up.

A certain amount of gearing is attractive to shareholders, for it should have the effect of raising their average real return on investment. A moderate amount of gearing involves borrowing at a level which presents little risk to the lenders. If the risk of default is low, the real interest rate should be low and in particular should be less than the real rate of return earned on equity. The shareholders therefore increase their average real return by cheap borrowing, but subject to the constraint that the borrowing will become more expensive if gearing becomes too high. By judicious gearing the shareholders achieve higher real returns for themselves at the expense of a small increase in the riskiness of their post-interest earnings.

This raises the question of what is meant by moderate gearing. A popular rule of thumb is that the gearing ratio should not exceed 40%, although some users of published accounts prefer to use 33% as their benchmark. This rule is reasonably sensible for typical British industrial concerns, although it should not be given too much authority. Gearing ratios are generally much higher in countries where financial markets follow a different pattern from the British one: in Germany and Japan companies usually obtain most of their long-term finance in the form of loans from banks, and gearing ratios of 75% are not unknown. Within Britain the acceptable level of gearing should always be decided by considering the degree of risk inherent in the company's trade. High gearing (eg, over 50%) is found in companies with a large proportion of their assets in land and buildings, such as property or hotel companies. The traditional view has been that such companies can be permitted higher than normal gearing because their asset base is very suitable as security for loans. This view has less force now, however, following the collapse in some property values during the 1970s, but it still has some validity in that property is still in general superior to plant and to stock as security for loans.

Gearing should be low where assets are unsuitable as security for loans and where operating earnings are very variable: in these risky trades it is necessary that the long-term finance should come almost entirely from equity. Some companies are contractually obliged to ensure that their gearing ratio does not exceed a given figure. This occurs where a company has issued debentures and the debenture trust deed limits the company's future long-term borrowings so that they shall not exceed some given fraction of shareholders' capital plus reserves. An arrangement of that sort protects the debenture holders from over-risky financial decisions by directors in the future.

When calculating a gearing ratio, the treatment of any preference share capital needs some thought. If the ratio is being calculated in order to inform judgments and decisions by long-term lenders, then the preference capital should be aggregated with equity and included with E in the $\frac{D}{D + E}$ ratio. This is because the creditor's claims take precedence over the preference claims on capital and income. However, if the ratio is being calculated to aid decisions and judgments by ordinary shareholders, the preference capital should be treated as debt and included with D in the $\frac{D}{D + E}$ calculation. This is done because, from the ordinary shareholder's point of view, both debenture holders and preference shareholders take precedence over him, and his entitlement is to the income left after both prior claims have been satisfied.

The effects of inflation must be allowed for in judging gearing, and three different ways of calculating $\frac{D}{D + E}$ can be distinguished. First, the figures for D and E can be obtained from an historical cost balance sheet. This will overestimate the true gearing ratio if assets, especially land, are included in the balance sheet at out-of-date values.

Second, the ratio can be calculated using a figure for E derived from a current cost balance sheet so that E represents capital and reserves, including the current cost reserve. The gearing ratio then measures shareholders' funds according to the current cost of the operating capacity presently owned by the company. (The figure for D would, of course, not be affected by the switch to the current cost measurement convention, unless the long-term loans had been indexed so that eventual capital repayments were linked to the inflation rate during the term of the loan.) This second method appears to be a better one to use and it is possible to use it for all companies within the scope of SSAP 16[2] since the standard requires a current cost balance sheet to be included in the annual report.

A third way in which the gearing ratio can be constructed involves using figures for D and E based on the current quoted prices of the company's securities. This method is popular in the United States, but it has its dangers. To illustrate this method a company is considered which has a financial structure including only 5 million £1 ordinary shares, quoted at £2, and £2 million of mortgage debentures quoted at 80. The market value of the equity is therefore £10 million and of the debentures is £1.6 million. The $\frac{D}{D + E}$ ratio is therefore $\frac{£1.6m}{£10m + £1.6m} = 14\%$.

It may be argued that this way of measuring gearing reflects current market opinions of the company's worth. However, the method can be dangerously misleading if there is any chance of a forced liquidation in the near future. It is true that the first two versions of the gearing ratio are also affected if the company should cease to be a going concern, because the potential liquidation values of assets will usually be substantially different from historical costs and from current costs. However, the third version of the gearing ratio, based on quoted prices for the company's securities, is particularly open to criticism. As the market becomes aware of a pending forced liquidation, the quoted price of the equity will fall, thereby raising the reported gearing ratio. Furthermore, the quoted price of the debentures may well rise towards their nominal value, eliminating the difference between the quoted price and the nominal value. This will occur because, provided the security for the debentures is sound, a buyer of debentures can

---

[2] ASC: Statement of Standard Accounting Practice No 16 Current Cost accounting, March 1980.

26

expect early repayment at 100. The pressure of buying power will thus cause the quoted debenture price in the example above to rise from 80 to 100.

In short, the effect of a pending forced liquidation will be a dramatic rise in the gearing ratio, if gearing is measured by the third method. The gearing ratio would appear to have changed very significantly, although no new borrowing has been undertaken and although the existing borrowing is fully secured and involves no risk of capital loss to the lenders. It can be seen that pending liquidation causes the third method to report a misleading value for the gearing ratio. The second method, based on current cost values, seems to provide a truer picture of gearing.

The problem of accounting for leases is important when considering gearing ratios. A company which obtains a sizeable proportion of its fixed assets by leasing them long term, rather than buying them, will appear to have a more favourable gearing ratio than an otherwise identical company which buys the fixed assets outright. The company which borrows long term and buys the assets will have the borrowing included with D in $\frac{D}{D + E}$ whilst the company which leases the assets will not have the obligation to meet future rentals included in D. The Accounting Standards Committee is moving towards a solution of this problem by suggesting in ED29[3] that lease commitments be capitalised and thereby included with borrowing in the gearing ratio. Until the ASC's standard on this is effective, users of the gearing ratio should apply the ratio warily when the company under examination has long-term lease commitments.

A final reservation to be kept in mind when assessing a gearing ratio is that the ratio is a static measure and it describes financial structure rather than financial flows. It can be that the gearing ratio appears very safe from perusal of the balance sheet but that doubt exists as to the company's ability to pay interest as it becomes due. Long-term creditors should therefore look at the interest cover ratio as well as the gearing ratio.

Interest cover ratio (or times interest earned)

Interest cover measures the company's debt-servicing capacity and provides a warning if there is some doubt as to whether the company can pay future interest on what it has borrowed.

The ratio is constructed by dividing the annual flow of income which is available to pay interest commitments by the interest due. The numerator is therefore the net profit before tax and before interest payable. Pre-tax profit, rather than post-tax profit, is used in the numerator because tax is only payable on

---

[3]   ASC: Exposure Draft No 29 Accounting for leases and hire purchase contracts, October 1981.

profits after interest, which is another way of saying that interest takes precedence over tax in the ranking of claims on operating earnings. The ratio measures the cover or safety margin for interest claims. The conventional wisdom requires that cover should be over 4 for safety, though the stability of cover over time is as important as the size of cover in a given year. A low cover figure warns creditors that there is a greater risk of non-payment of interest should there be any future fall in operating earnings.

The interest cover can be calculated in various ways, either measuring the cover for each fixed long-term interest charge (eg, cover for the 10% first mortgage debentures) or measuring the cover for unsecured short-term interest or the cover for all interest.

Interest cover can be calculated using either current cost profit (before interest and tax) or historical cost profit. The former ratio shows the cover available for interest charges without the company reducing its operating capacity. It therefore measures the company's ability to service its borrowing whilst still maintaining its long-term viability and its ability to produce a given volume of goods or services. On the other hand, the historical cost interest cover is closer to a cash-based indication of cover. The historical cost profit in the numerator of the ratio shows the surplus earned for lenders, the tax authorities and the share-holders, and this surplus is measured after maintaining capital in money terms. Under this convention no regard is paid to the effect of rising prices on the finance needed to maintain operating capacity: attention is concentrated on the legal position, which is that the interest must be paid when due, and tax liabilities (based principally on historical cost profit) must be paid. In short, it is the historical cost profit which measures the position as far as suppliers and lenders are concerned.

Of the two versions of the interest cover ratio the current cost version can therefore be interpreted as a long-term measure of the company's ability to service debt whilst maintaining its relative importance in the economy. The historical cost cover shows the short-term position. It will often be found that a company shows high cover on the historical cost basis but low, or negative, cover on the current cost basis. (This is so because, with continued price rises in operating assets, the current cost profit will invariably be less than historical cost profit.) Looking at these cover figures the lender to the company would fairly conclude that future interest payments seemed secure on a short-term cash basis but that the company appeared likely to decline in the long term in terms of operating capacity because it would be dissipating its real capital in future interest payments and losses.

An interesting point to consider is whether the current cost profit to be used in the interest cover ratio should be taken before or after the gearing adjustment. This issue can be illustrated using an extract from the current cost profit statement of Courtaulds for the year to March 1982:

		£m	
Historical cost trading profit			71
Current cost operating adjustments			46
			—
Current cost operating profit			25
Interest payable	£m	22	
Gearing adjustment		(14)	8
			—
			17

The interest cover is well over 3 on a historical basis, but the question is whether the current cost cover for the interest payments is best indicated by £25m (the c.c. operating profit) or by £39m (the operating profit after the gearing adjustment). The purpose of the gearing adjustment is to reflect the fact that Courtauld's shareholders have financed only 70% of its operating capacity and the other 30% has been financed by borrowings. Therefore, the proponents of the gearing adjustment would argue, the shareholders only need to bear 70% of the £46m operating adjustments. This is achieved by debiting £14m (ie, 30% of £46m) to current cost reserve and crediting it to the profits available to the shareholders for possible distribution. The gearing adjustment is therefore an internal transfer amongst the shareholders' funds, designed to provide guidance for decisions on dividend policy. It guides directors as to how much can be paid out as dividend while maintaining the same operating capacity, assuming the company can maintain the same ratio of borrowings. But the gearing adjustment does not affect the operating profit, which is the stream of income from which interest must be met. It may be concluded therefore that the numerator of the current cost version of interest cover should be current cost operating earnings before tax, before interest and before the gearing adjustment.

Some companies have enormous interest cover. Great Universal Stores offered its creditors cover of over 50 in 1980 on a historical cost basis and just under 50 on a current cost basis. An example of a much lower figure is provided by Godfrey Davis, which had a policy of relatively heavy borrowing secured on its fleet of hire cars. Interest cover in the 1980 accounts was 2.8 on a historical cost basis and 1.9 on a current cost basis. These figures might be thought to be on the low side though, to a great extent, they reflect management policy and the distinguishing features of the trade.

In conclusion, the interest cover ratio, like the gearing ratio, indicates the degree of risk to which lenders to the company are exposed. The difference between the ratios is that the gearing ratio looks at relative amounts of finance at a point in time, whilst the interest cover looks at flows of money over a period of time. Also, the gearing ratio is like a golf handicap in that a low figure is desirable, whilst interest cover is like an examination mark in that a high figure is desirable, where "desirable" indicates low risk for the lender.

3 Ratios derived from Consolidated Accounts

It has been assumed so far that the reader of financial accounting statements has been interested in the results and the liquidity of a single company. Users of accounts often find, however, that the company in which they are interested is a member of a group of companies. In these circumstances the holding company of the group is obliged by the Companies Act 1948 to produce group accounts, and this obligation is in practice usually satisfied by the holding company issuing consolidated accounts. In these consolidated accounts the activities, assets and liabilities of the entire group are portrayed together, as if the group were a single entity. It is natural therefore for the ratio user to attempt to judge the group's performance and financial position by calculating ratios from these consolidated accounts.

The usefulness of ratios derived from consolidated accounts depends on the nature of the ratio user's interest in the group. A shareholder in the holding company will usually find such ratios helpful. However, a creditor of the holding company should use group ratios with caution. For example, a trade creditor of the holding company might note with satisfaction that the group's liquid ratio is over 2. However, it could be that this merely indicates that for every pound owed to short-term British creditors two pounds of liquid assets were held by a subsidiary in an overseas territory where local exchange control laws banned any remittances to the UK. In these circumstances the group's liquidity ratio, considered on its own, gives a misleading view of short-term liquid cover for the trade creditors' claims. Generally the creditor of the holding company will need to calculate ratios from the holding company's own accounts as well as from the consolidated accounts. In the case of minority shareholders and creditors of a subsidiary, the group ratios will be of very little relevance, for the position of these parties depends on the particular subsidiary they are concerned with. If that subsidiary is in difficulties, the holding company may decide not to come to its rescue, and so assets and profits elsewhere in the group are not available to claimants against the subsidiary in question. In general, therefore, it may be said that consolidated ratios are primarily for the use of shareholders in the holding company.

Users of consolidated ratios should be aware of the accounting practices required in consolidations by the Companies Acts and by SSAP 14[1]. The ratio user can assume that uniform accounting practices are used throughout the group and that a common balance sheet date has been adopted, unless the notes to the accounts give a warning to the contrary. He can also assume that the conventional accounting practices have been applied in reporting such matters as goodwill arising on consolidation (or premium on acquisition, as it is called in SSAP 14), minority interests, profits of subsidiaries earned before and after they joined the group, unrealised profits arising on transactions within the group and the setting-off of assets and liabilities.

The ratio user should construct the consolidated ratios along the same lines as he would for a company, taking care that the coverage of the numerator and denominator are consistent. For example, in a return on capital ratio the reward of the minorities and their investment should be included in numerator and denominator respectively or, alternatively, they should be excluded from both. Generally, it will be more useful to exclude the minorities, thereby showing the return on the investment of shareholders in the holding company.

The interpretation of consolidated ratios requires extra care in three circumstances – where there are foreign subsidiaries, where merger accounting has been adopted and where the group has associates.

Foreign subsidiaries

A subsidiary operating overseas will, of course, use its own domestic currency for its trading activities and for preparing its accounts. On the balance sheet date the subsidiary's accounts will have to be translated to sterling for incorporation in the consolidated accounts. British holding companies traditionally used the temporal (or historical rate) method for translating the accounts of overseas subsidiaries into sterling. That method, being based on the view that the subsidiary's trade was an extension of the parent's, translated the subsidiary's assets and liabilities at the exchange rate which prevailed when the asset/liability was acquired. The method resulted in the consolidated profit and loss account being credited/charged with profits/losses arising as a result of changes in the exchange rate. Generally, if sterling rose relative to the subsidiary's currency, the group profit statement included a foreign exchange profit and, correspondingly, if sterling weakened, the group profits were reduced. (The foregoing is valid provided local borrowings exceed current assets, as would usually be the case.) The traditional British attachment to the temporal method has changed in the last two decades, chiefly

[1] ASC: Statement of Standard Accounting Practice No 14 Group accounts, September 1978.

because subsidiaries now tend to operate more independently and to raise capital locally. The overseas subsidiary is now more often regarded as a trading entity separate from its holding company, with some measure of autonomy in its trading and financing decisions. The holding company's stake in the subsidiary is therefore regarded as an investment in the subsidiary, rather than an investment in the subsidiary's net assets. The accounting method which reflects this view is the closing rate (or net investment) method. The overwhelming majority of British holding companies now use the closing rate method and this method is required by SSAP 20[2] except in cases where the foreign subsidiary's trade is more dependent on the economic environment of sterling than on that of its own foreign currency (in which case the temporal method should be used). The closing rate method translates the subsidiary's assets and liabilities at the exchange rate prevailing on the balance sheet date, with no regard to the exchange rate which prevailed when the subsidiary acquired its assets. The foreign exchange surplus or deficit which arises on consolidation is then taken directly to reserve and not passed through the profit statement; in particular it will not affect earnings per share.

The ratio user should therefore be careful when comparing the performance ratios of two groups of companies since he will be making an invalid comparison if one group uses the closing rate method whilst the other uses the temporal method. The extent to which the ratio comparison is misleading will depend on the relative stability of exchange rates – the comparison will be more misleading if the subsidiaries operate in countries with very high inflation rates (and therefore with rapidly weakening exchange rates) than if they operate in countries whose exchange rates against sterling show only minor fluctuations.

Apart from the problem of translating the accounts of overseas subsidiaries into sterling, there is the separate problem that the local currency of a subsidiary may not be freely convertible into sterling. The subsidiary may be subject to exchange or trade controls, to legal limits on the payment of dividends or to penal taxation if it remits profits to the holding company. SSAP 14 requires that any significant restrictions on the holding company's ability to distribute the retained profits of the group should be disclosed in the consolidated accounts. However, even where there are no restrictions on subsidiaries remitting dividends to the holding company, there are often restrictions on capital movements, and the reader of the consolidated accounts cannot in general assume that group assets are fully transferable across national boundaries to satisfy group liabilities. It follows that the ratios measuring solvency, liquidity and financial structure are of very limited value when based on a consolidated balance sheet incorporating foreign subsidiaries.

---

[2]   ASC: Statement of Standard Accounting Practice No 20 Foreign currency translation, April 1983.

Merger accounting

Ratios based on consolidated accounts will generally be affected by whether the group's accounting policy is to use acquisition accounting or merger accounting. Acquisition accounting involves (1) freezing the pre-acquisition profits of the subsidiary, which are not treated as available for distribution; (2) revaluing the underlying assets of the acquired subsidiary; and (3) accounting for the share premium which arises when the holding company issues its shares to acquire the subsidiary. Merger accounting (or pooling of interests) offers an alternative way of presenting the consolidated accounts which the Companies Act 1981 permits when the holding company owns 90% of the subsidiary's shares, subject to certain other conditions being satisfied. (The 1981 Act also contains retrospective provisions which permit some holding companies to continue to use merger accounting for mergers undertaken before 4 February 1981, even although the 90% condition is not met. Also Exposure Draft 31[3] sets out the conditions which should be met for the merger accounting alternative to be used). Under merger accounting (1) pre-acquisition profits of the subsidiary are not frozen; (2) the underlying assets are consolidated at book value (not revalued); and (3) no share premium arises.

Merger accounting has been criticised as "creative accounting" because it tends to give a less prudent view of the group's performance than does acquisition accounting. For example, the adoption of merger accounting will tend to cause an apparent improvement in return on shareholders' capital: the numerator, profit, is increased because depreciation is based on book values rather than on revaluations, whilst the denominator is reduced because the premium on the newly issued shares is not accounted for. There is also more scope for the holding company to increase its dividend because the consolidated profit and loss account includes the pre-acquisition profits of the subsidiary.

The ratio user should therefore always read the accounting policies of the group to see whether acquisition or merger accounting is used. He should keep in mind the fact that merger accounting tends to give a more favourable set of performance ratios than acquisition accounting.

Associate companies

A group of companies will in practice very often have associate companies as well as subsidiaries, and therefore the ratio user needs to be aware of the way in which consolidated ratios are affected by the profits and the assets of

[3]   ASC: Exposure Draft No 31 Accounting for mergers and acquisitions, October 1982.

associates. SSAP 1[4] defines an associated company. Put simply, it is a company, not being a subsidiary, over which the holding company can exercise a significant influence because it has a long-term, substantial shareholding or because it is effectively a partner in a joint venture. A shareholding of 20% or more is deemed to amount to significant influence unless the contrary can be clearly demonstrated. In broad terms, therefore, a company will generally be an associate if between 20% and 50% of its shares are held by the holding company. The effect of associate status is that the consolidated accounts will include the group's share of the associate's profits rather than merely the dividends receivable from the associate. In the consolidated balance sheet the investment in associates will appear at cost, plus the group's share of post-acquisition retained profits, less any amounts written off.

The effect of a company being deemed to be an associate will usually be to make the consolidated ratios look more favourable. For example, suppose the holding company increases its stake in another company from 19½% to 20%, thereby raising the presumption that the latter company is an associate. The first effect will be that the consolidated profit and loss account will include 20% of the associate's profits instead of merely 19½% of the associate's *distributed* profits. This effect will naturally be greater where the associate has high dividend cover. The result will be an improvement in the group's earnings per share and its return on capital.

The consolidated gearing ratio can also be "improved" by judicious use of associate company accounting, and the ratio user should take care that he is not misled by this. For example, the holding company might own 51% of the shares in a subsidiary which has very substantial borrowings. The whole of these borrowings would appear in the consolidated balance sheet and might thereby cause the group gearing to look embarrassingly high. If the directors decide to reduce their stake in the subsidiary to 50%, it will be reclassified as an associate, and then *none* of its borrowings will appear in the group balance sheet. The effect of the relatively trivial sale of 1% of the former subsidiary's shares might therefore lead to a substantial reduction in the group's apparent gearing. The ratio user is to some extent protected by the tightening up in the definition of an associate contained in the 1982 revision of SSAP 1. He should furthermore ensure that he reads the accounts thoroughly and notes any changes in the list of associates during the group's accounting year.

In summary, the ratios derived from consolidated accounts are useful to shareholders in the holding company, but of limited use to persons with other types of interest in the group. Those who use consolidated ratios should be aware of the effects of consolidation accounting practices, in particular the practices used for translating foreign currencies, for accounting for mergers and for incorporating the results of associates.

---

[4] ASC: Statement of Standard Accounting Practice No 1 Accounting for associated companies, issued January 1971, amended August 1974, revised April 1982.

4 The Dangers of Ratio Analysis

Ratio analysis is a useful tool for those who base decisions on financial accounts. However, the tool is sometimes dangerous, for it can mislead decision makers and result in bad decisions. Among the dangers of using ratio analysis are those arising when the ratio user:

- ignores a company's accounting policies;
- disregards the peculiarities of the company's trade;
- makes improper comparisons;
- makes technical accounting errors in constructing ratios;
- relies exclusively on ratios.

We now deal with these dangers in turn.

Accounting policies

Ratio users should heed the warning often given to computer users: "Garbage in – garbage out!" If the raw data fed into a computing system is wrong, the output will be misleading. Similarly the reliability of a ratio is no better than that of the accounting figures comprising its numerator and denominator. These two figures will usually be affected by the accounting policies adopted by the company in such matters as valuation of land and buildings, depreciation charges, treatment of goodwill and research and development costs, stock valuation, bad debt provisions, deferred tax provisions, capitalisation of lease commitments, and so on. In particular one or both of the figures may be distorted by the historical cost convention in times of inflation.

The ratio user may be misled if he ignores changes of accounting policy by a company. For example, a company's current cost return on total assets might fall from 10% in 1981 to 5% in 1982 merely because the directors have decided that the 1982 accounts should follow the proposals in ED29[1] for capitalising assets held under finance leases.

The ratio user can also be misled if he compares the ratios of two companies which use dissimilar accounting policies. For example, one might conclude that company A was better managed than its competitors B because A's return on capital was higher. But this difference in ratios might be due to a decision by the directors of B to provide for deferred taxation in full whilst A's directors have merely disclosed the potential deferred taxation position in a note to the accounts (as is permitted by SSAP 15[2], provided A is a going concern and reversal of the timing differences is unlikely during the next three years). The true position, which will be revealed by amending the profits of A and B so that they are calculated on a comparable basis, might be that B is better managed and more profitable than A. This danger is especially great if the two companies are incorporated in different countries, since then it is highly likely that accounting policy differences will exist. This is because the international standardisation of financial accounting (through the International Accounting Standards Committee) is less advanced than domestic standardisation within the British Isles (through the ASC). Some nations are not members of the IASC, some do not take active steps to enforce international standards and some disagree with particular international standards and devise their own national standards at variance with the international ones.

The most extreme form of error over accounting policies would be to compare a current cost ratio of one company with a historical cost ratio of another.

The way to avoid these dangers is to read the notes to the accounts and to make comparisons only between ratios constructed from figures which are based on similar accounting policies. Where additional information is available from the companies under investigation, it is quite possible to construct fully comparable ratios. This is the main task undertaken by the Centre for Interfirm Comparison, which has over twenty years of experience in deriving comparable ratios for companies which do not use the same accounting policies. Where such additional information is not available the ratio user can sometimes achieve the necessary adjustments from the published accounts and notes to the accounts, taken together. In other cases a choice must be made between using estimates or refraining from ratio comparisons.

Peculiarities of the trade

Before basing decisions on ratios one should be quite clear as to the nature of the

---

[1] ASC: Exposure Draft No 29 Accounting for leases and hire purchase contracts, October 1981.
[2] ASC: Statement of Standard Accounting Practice No 15 Accounting for deferred taxation, October 1978.

trade the company carries on. The very minimum would be to read the statement of principal activities of the company in the directors' report. The ratio user should consider why the company has chosen the date used for the accounting year-end and whether the trade is seasonal, or steady throughout the year. The year-end may have been chosen because of seasonal factors – for example, because stock is at its lowest point (and so stocktaking is then quick and costs of stocktaking are minimised) or because tourism is then at a low ebb or because a crop has been harvested. In trades with seasonal fluctuations the year-end figures for stocks, debtors and creditors may all give a false impression of their average values over the year. It follows that ratios based on these untypical figures will be equally misleading.

For example, consider a company which manufactures Christmas cards steadily through the year and sells them all to wholesalers each November. Its stock turnover ratio, calculated from a balance sheet on 31 December, will give the impression of fairly rapid turnover since stocks will be low on that date. In fact the true stock turnover will be very slow because stock will on average be held for six months before sale. In these circumstances one should either obtain monthly stock figures or refrain from using the stock turnover ratio.

Related to this matter of seasonal cycles is the issue of longer-term variations. Some companies will, from the nature of their trade, experience uneven earnings over the years due to exchange rate risks, crop yields which are affected by drought and disease, or other unpredictable but possibly recurring factors. The effects of these factors will show up as profit fluctuations attributable to extra-ordinary and exceptional profits and losses. SSAP 6[3] defines extraordinary items as those which derive from events or transactions outside the ordinary activities of the business and which are both material and expected not to recur frequently or regularly. Exceptional items are unusual on account of size and incidence (and may therefore require separate disclosure) but derive from the ordinary activities of the business. Judgments of company ratios should be made with care where extraordinary or exceptional items are disclosed. An example is provided by the accounts of Allied Breweries. The group's results for the year to 3 March, 1981 were:

Current cost profit available for ordinary shareholders	£m	26.9
Less Extraordinary items (costs of closures, redundancies and reorganisations)		25.3
	£m	1.6

---

[3] ASC: Statement of Standard Accounting Practice No 6 Extraordinary items and prior year adjustments, April 1974 with a new part 5 added June 1978.

Since the ordinary shareholders' funds on a current cost basis were £1,001m at the start of the year, the ratio of return on ordinary capital is 2.69% or 0.16%, depending on which profit figure is used as the numerator. The danger is that an unthinking ratio user might rely on the 0.16% figure without realising the extraordinary nature of the closure costs and their materiality.

Some trades have characteristics which will modify the usual meanings given to standard terms such as fixed and current assets. Fixed assets can be defined as assets held for their service potential whilst current assets are those which will be consumed and/or converted into cash through sales in the ordinary course of business. In practice, users of accounts assume that fixed assets are held long term whilst current assets are fairly quickly converted to cash, and usually this assumption is a justified extension of the definitions. However, in some industries these extensions may be wrong. For example, a car-hire company will properly treat its fleet of hire cars as fixed assets but it may sell each car as soon as it is one year old, so that fixed assets are not held long term. Also a distillery will properly treat its maturing whisky as a current asset even although it will not be sold for perhaps five years. Where the trade concerned has these unusual characteristics the ratio user should treat the ratios with caution. He should not interpret the distillery's current ratio as a measure of short-term asset cover for short-term liabilities. And he should not condemn the car-hire firm for breaking the prudent rule which says: "Do not use short-term borrowing to finance fixed assets".

As a final illustration of the need to consider the peculiarities of a company's trade when judging its ratios, consider the following large Scottish company. Its accounts pubished in 1980 showed profit before interest and taxes of £190 million, of which interest took £150 million. Interest cover was therefore only 1.3. This sounds like a danger sign if the conventional rule of thumb for judging interest cover is used, especially as interest cover had fallen from the previous year's figure of 1.4. The unthinking ratio user might decide that the company was heading for trouble and perhaps liquidation, and he might take steps to avoid becoming an unsecured creditor of the company. In fact our ratio user need have no fears, for the company is the Bank of Scotland, and its ratios are prudent by the standards appropriate to a clearing bank. The point of this illustration is that the ratio user should be aware of the nature of the company's trade and should not use the ratios which are normal for industrial companies for judging banks, property or insurance companies, long-term contractors, hotels, and so on.

The requirement for awareness of the nature of the trade implies, of course, that any changes in the trade carried on should be allowed for, whether they are qualitative or quantitative changes. To illustrate a large quantitative change: on 1 April 1980 Racal, with sharehholders' funds of £128 million, acquired Decca for £106 million after an energetic take-over battle. In the absence of knowledge about this change, an unthinking ratio user might compare Racal's ratios from its 1980 and 1981 accounts and make misleading inferences: he should, of course, read the chairman's statement, directors' report and notes to the accounts to supplement the bare ratios.

Improper comparisons

The purpose of calculating a ratio is often to compare it with the same ratio for other companies. This raises the question of how one identifies a comparable company. The starting point is the crude industrial classification of the company and this can usually be taken a step further by reading the statement of principal activities in the directors' report. Even this elementary information gives the ratio user some help in identifying comparable companies. Perusal of directors' reports shows, for example, that Great Universal Stores is active in catalogue mail order whilst British Home Stores restricts its activities to chain stores. The ratios of these two retailers are not, therefore, directly comparable. The crude classification of industries can be deceptive, as in the case of companies in the brewing industry: companies like Scottish & Newcastle, Allied and Guinness tend on average to derive about one-quarter of their turnover from non-brewing activities. Conglomerates provide the extreme example of such diversification and therefore the greatest problems in ratio comparability.

Even within a given industrial classification, and assuming no diversification, comparability is difficult. The Centre for Interfirm Comparison has devised a classification system based on the range and nature of company products and the pattern of sales. For example, within engineering, companies which offer a range of standard products from stock are naturally not comparable with companies which offer to manufacture customer-designed products after receipt of orders. Ingham and Taylor Harrington[4] have clearly explained the CFIC system.

The review of some of the problems of identifying comparable companies shows that a scale of variation is involved. At one end of the scale there may be two companies which are almost identical in the nature of their trade. At the other end there may be two totally dissimilar companies (*eg*, one a travel agent, the other an agricultural engineering concern). Now if the ratios of two closely comparable companies are compared, conclusions can be drawn as to efficiency and managerial competence. Suppose, for example, that the ratio user is considering two engineering companies which are very similar in their activities and which adopt the same accounting and financial policies. If one of the companies shows a consistent current cost return on capital of 10%, whilst the other consistently earns only 8%, this suggests that the former company is probably more efficient and its management is making better decisions. However, if the ratios of two very dissimilar companies are compared, conclusions cannot be drawn as to efficiency

[4]   Ingham, H. and Taylor Harrington, L.: "Interfirm comparison", Heinemann, 1980.

and the quality of management. The comparison may still be worth making for other reasons, such as to judge creditworthiness, but it would be improper to interpret differences in efficiency terms. The differences could well be due to trade characteristics or to factors quite outside the control of management. It could be that the return on capital of the electronics exporting company is lower than that of the domestic road transport company because the former is hampered by a high foreign exchange value of sterling, and the board of the former company can hardly be blamed for that.

In summary, the general rule is that where companies are very similar their ratios can be compared as an aid to all categories of decisions. But where companies are dissimilar the purposes for which ratio comparison is proper are more circumscribed. It is still appropriate to compare ratios for credit risk assessment and investment potential, but it is improper to compare ratios to judge relative efficiency and relative management ability.

Technical errors

A financial ratio can naturally mislead if it is erroneously constructed. The important point here is the compatibility of numerator and denominator. It has already been stressed that the user of ratios derived from consolidated accounts must pay due attention to the treatment of minority interests in numerator and denominator. In a return on capital ratio, minority interests should either be included or excluded. It is not proper to include their share of profits in the numerator whilst excluding their investment from the denominator, and vice versa.

Putting this more generally, the definitions of numerator and denominator must be compatible in that their coverage must be the same. A non-accounting example may help to bring out the principle involved. If a demographer wishes to calculate the birth rate he could divide the figure for births in Scotland in 1981 by the average Scottish population during the year. Alternatively he could calculate the ratio for the whole of the UK. What he should not do is divide Scottish births by total UK population, for the resultant ratio would be nonsense. The point is obvious in the demographic example given, yet a similar error can be made with financial ratios. It has been claimed that the ratio of profit to *total* assets is useful. But this ratio is meaningless. One should either divide profit (the shareholders' reward) by shareholders' funds, or one should divide profit plus interest paid (*ie*, the reward of shareholders plus the reward of creditors) by total assets (which represent the funds of shareholders and creditors). Both ratios can be useful. A hybrid ratio which includes creditors' (interest-bearing) finance in the denominator but excludes creditors' rewards from the numerator is useless.

Exclusive reliance on ratios

A claim was made in the Preface that ratio analysis is useful for dispelling the feelings of helplessness experienced by the reader of accounts who is faced with a mass of detailed information. Ratios help by compressing the detail to understandable proportions and they guide users to asking the right questions and hence to making better business decisions. Each of these claims can be verified by watching the business and financial community go about its daily work. However, whilst ratio analysis offers help and guidance, it is not a magic panacea. Business decisions should never be based solely on financial ratios. The preceding sections have contained several illustrations of cases where reliance on a ratio will be misleading if the ratio user has not read the notes to the accounts and the directors' report. Particular emphasis has been given to the need for awareness both of the accounting policies used and of the nature of the company's trade. There are many other matters on which the ratio user should inform himself, and the task of doing so has become easier over the years as disclosure requirements have improved and as accounting standards have been introduced.

Perusal of the notes to the accounts will inform the ratio user of contingent liabilities and capital commitments. This data is very much to the point when considering the current and liquid ratios because an apparently satisfactory ratio would be vulnerable if a new liability were to arise at an early date to swell the current liabilities figure in the ratio. Notes dealing with contingencies often make interesting reading: examples in recent years include the claims against Distillers arising from Thalidomide, and the Zambian government's claim for over £3,000 million from Shell and some associates for alleged conspiracy to supply oil to what was then Rhodesia. SSAP 18[5] requires that material contingent losses which are probable should be provided for, and that other material contingent losses should be mentioned in a note unless the possibility of loss is remote.

A further reason for the ratio user to read the notes to the accounts is that he may find in the notes disclosures regarding window dressing. This objectionable practice involves the undertaking of transactions just before the balance sheet date, and the subsequent reversal or maturity of these transactions shortly after the balance sheet date in circumstances where the primary purpose of these transactions is to alter the appearance of the balance sheet. Window dressing therefore involves a deliberate attempt to obscure the true and fair view which the accounts should give. As an exaggerated example of this practice, suppose a company has on its accounting date £2 million of current liabilities but liquid assets of only £1 million. The company has a dangerously low liquid ratio. To conceal this the directors might borrow £1 million just before the balance sheet date, holding

---

[5] ASC: Statement of Standard Accounting Practice No 18 Accounting for contingencies, August 1980.

the proceeds of the loan in cash on that date but repaying the loan after a few days. The liquid ratio would thereby be raised from its true figure of 0.5 to 0.66. Ratio users are protected in these circumstances by SSAP 17[6] on accounting for post balance sheet events, which requires disclosure of window dressing transactions in the notes to the accounts.

Whilst SSAP 17 will protect the ratio user from being deceived by window dressing, there are still numerous ways in which the ratio user may make incorrect inferences due to the limitations which are inevitable in a system of annual accounting. The case of a department store provides one illustration of these limitations. It is accepted that stocktaking is an expensive task in such a store and that it is expedient to undertake it when stock is at the lowest point of the annual cycle, which will often be just after the January sales. A department store may therefore choose 31 January as its year end. This practice has the disadvantage that the balance sheet reveals an untypically low stock figure, but the practice is adopted on cost grounds, is widely used and is generally well understood. Another illustration is where a company deliberately undertakes a sales campaign just before its year-end in order to reduce the reported stock figure in the balance sheet and thereby to improve its liquid ratio. The same effect can be observed if the sales campaign has a different motive: it could be due to the marketing manager's concern that he is not going to be able to meet his annual sales target. For example, it is not unknown for a life insurance company to use its sales incentive scheme to put pressure on salesmen to sign up the maximum number of new policyholders just before the year-end, thereby boosting the year's figures for new policies written.

These illustrations do not involve window dressing because there is no intent to deceive. The sales campaign in the final months of the financial year may have been motivated by the need to be able to show acceptable results in the balance sheet but this motivation does not alter the fact that sales were achieved, stock was reduced, and the accounts give a true and fair view of what was achieved in the year and of the end-of-year position. The ratio user may still draw incorrect inferences as to the department store's average stock, or as to the life office's month-by-month figures for new policies written, but these incorrect inferences cannot be attributed to window dressing. They would be due to the ratio user's ignorance of the inevitable limitations of annual accounts.

In the notes to the accounts the ratio user will also find information on loan expiry which should be considered alongside the liquidity ratios. A company whose liquid and current ratios are on the low side will cause even more concern should an outstanding loan be due for repayment, say, fifteen months after the balance sheet date. On the other hand, a similar company whose loans still have

---

[6] ASC: Statement of Standard Accounting Practice No 17 Accounting for post balance sheet events, August 1980.

fifteen years to go before repayment will appear to be in less danger of a liquidity crisis.

As well as reading all the notes to the accounts the ratio user should read the audit report, since, if the accounts do not give a true and fair view, neither will the ratios derived from them. The worst that could be found from the ratio viewpoint would probably be a going concern qualification. If the auditor is not satisfied that the company can continue trading for the foreseeable future then ratios derived from accounting figures based on the going concern assumption will often be worthless, since the realisable values of stocks and fixed assets on a forced liquidation will often be but a fraction of book value. Redundancy payments would also arise as new liabilities.

It has been stressed that ratios should be judged bearing in mind the information in notes to the accounts and the directors' report. This point can be made more general by extending the range of additional information. First, the non-accounting content of the company's annual report may throw a different light on the ratios. For example, a satisfactory return on capital may have been earned, but the annual report may show that key directors are leaving the company, and their leaving may cast doubt on future profitability. Second, the ratios should not be relied upon to the exclusion of sources of information independent of the annual report. A prudent potential creditor will not judge the company's creditworthiness solely from its accounts (especially if it is a small company) but will rely on references and commercial credit ratings, such as those of Dun and Bradstreet. As an illustration, suppose a bank manager were approached for a loan by a small company. The usefulness of the solvency ratios to the bank manager would be somewhat overshadowed by the discovery that a senior manager in the company had a criminal conviction for fraud!

The final danger of ratio analysis is that it relates only to the company's past, but it is the future with which ratio users are usually concerned. Ratios should, therefore, be used in conjunction with any forecasts which can be made as to the future of the company and the industry in which it operates. Decision makers who use ratios should bear in mind that the ratios may have been made irrelevant by subsequent drastic changes in market conditions, laws, import duties, taxes, exchange rates, and so on.

Conclusion

Ratio analysis has its dangers, but a knowledge of these dangers should help the user to avoid them. The ratio user should inform himself about the company's accounting policies and the nature of its trade, and he should not rely exclusively on the ratios when making decisions. Subject to these qualifications, ratios are a valuable tool for assessing a business.

Appendix

This Appendix shows extracts from a recent annual report of the Scottish & Newcastle Breweries group. It then goes on to show how ratios may be constructed from these accounts to measure profitability and performance, and also liquidity, solvency and financial structure.

SCOTTISH & NEWCASTLE BREWERIES LIMITED

Group profit and loss statement (historical cost basis) for the 52 weeks ended May 1, 1983

	1983 £m	1982 £m
Turnover	641.8	620.5
Operating profit	52.0	47.8
Financial income	2.8	2.4
	54.8	50.2
Less: Financial expenses	13.7	18.0
Profit before taxation	41.1	32.2
Less: Taxation	14.2	9.7
Profit after taxation	26.9	22.5
Less: Extraordinary items	—	3.4
Attributable to Scottish & Newcastle Breweries Ltd.	26.9	19.1
Less: Preference dividends	0.5	0.5
Attributable to ordinary shareholders	26.4	18.6
Less: Ordinary dividends	13.2	12.4
Profit retained	13.2	6.2

APPENDIX

Group balance sheet (historical cost basis) at May 1, 1983

	1983 £m	1982 £m
Capital employed		
Ordinary capital	56.4	56.4
Reserves	271.7	258.5
	328.1	314.9
Preference capital	10.9	10.9
Loan capital	102.1	110.5
Deferred taxation	1.1	0.7
	442.2	437.0
Assets employed		
Land, buildings, plant and equipment	372.5	367.6
Investments	1.3	1.3
Fixed assets	373.8	368.9
Loans to customers	49.4	49.0
Current assets		
Stocks	63.5	64.0
Debtors	82.4	80.7
Cash and short term investments	7.6	10.0
	153.5	154.7
Current liabilities		
Creditors	103.3	92.3
Bank overdrafts and short term borrowings	11.8	30.1
Taxation	10.5	5.1
Dividends	8.9	8.1
	134.5	135.6
Net current assets	19.0	19.1
	442.2	437.0

Group current cost profit and loss statement for the 52 weeks ended May 1, 1983

	£m	£m
Turnover		641.8
Operating profit as shown in historical cost accounts		52.0
Deduct: Current cost operating adjustments		
Depreciation	11.5	
Cost of sales	4.5	
Monetary working capital	(2.0)	14.0
Current cost operating profit		38.0
Financial expenses (net)	10.9	
Gearing adjustment	(2.0)	8.9
Current cost profit before taxation		29.1
Less: Taxation		14.2
Current cost profit after taxation		14.9
Less: Preference dividends		0.5
Current cost profit attributable to ordinary shareholders		14.4
Less: Ordinary dividends		13.2
Transfer to reserves		1.2

APPENDIX

Group current cost balance sheet at May 1, 1983

	£m
Capital employed	
Ordinary capital	56.4
Current cost reserve	112.7
Other reserves	237.0
	406.1
Preference capital	10.9
Loan capital	102.1
Deferred taxation	1.1
	520.2
Assets employed	
Land, buildings, plant and equipment	441.9
Investments	5.6
Fixed assets	447.5
Loans to customers	49.4
Net current assets	
Stocks	67.9
Monetary working capital liabilities (net)	(15.0)
	52.9
Dividends	(8.9)
Other current liabilities (net)	(20.7)
	23.3
	520.2

RATIOS MEASURING PROFITABILITY AND PERFORMANCE

Return on Capital
Historical cost return on equity capital:
    The numerator is net profit available to ordinary shareholders, after interest, taxation, extraordinary items and preference dividends *ie* £26.4m
    The denominator is the opening or average figure for ordinary shareholders' funds. There have been no changes in issued capital during the year, so it is simpler to use the opening figure.

Historical cost return on capital was therefore $\dfrac{£\ 26.4m}{£314.9m} = 8.4\%$

When considering this ratio and making comparisons with other companies it is important to bear in mind that the "historical cost" balance sheet of Scottish & Newcastle includes the group's tied estates, which are revalued from time to time. For example, in 1982 the book value of such property rose by almost £50m due to such revaluations. Therefore the figure of £314.9m in the above ratio is not the true historical cost of equity assets. It is rather a value intermediate between the historical cost and the current cost of the equity assets.
Current cost return on equity capital:
    The numerator is the net current cost profit available for ordinary shareholders *ie* £14.4m
    The denominator should be the opening or average ordinary shareholders' funds. The opening current cost balance sheet is not reproduced in this appendix but it showed the opening value of ordinary shareholders' funds to be £409.7m. (This corresponds to the closing figure of £406.1m which is reproduced above).

Therefore the current cost return on equity capital was $\dfrac{£\ 14.4m}{£409.7m} = 3.5\%$

Profit to Sales
Historical cost profit to sales:
    Using operating profit as the numerator, the ratios are

    1982 $\dfrac{£\ 47.8m}{£620.5m} = 7.7\%$

    1983 $\dfrac{£\ 52.0m}{£641.8m} = 8.1\%$

Current cost profit to sales:
    Using current cost operating profit as the numerator:

$$1983 \quad \frac{£ \ 38.0m}{£641.8m} = 5.9\%$$

In the case of a brewery group it can be argued that the operating profit in the above numerators should be augmented by the financial income (which was £2.8m in 1983). This financial income arises largely from loans to free trade customers, which are made for trading purposes rather than as pure financial investments.

Sales to capital
Using historical cost total assets at the start of the year:

$$\frac{£641.8m}{£368.9m + £49.0m + £154.7m} = 1.12$$

Using current cost total assets: the total assets at the end of the year are used, because the opening figure is not reproduced here. The current cost balance sheet discloses that fixed assets were £447.5m, loans to customers were £49.4m and stocks were £67.9m. Other current assets were debtors and cash totalling £90m (this is obtained from the historical cost balance sheet). Therefore total assets at current cost were the sum of these four figures *ie*, £654.8m

$$\text{Therefore sales to current cost total assets} = \frac{£641.8m}{£654.8m} = 0.98$$

Value added to sales
Scottish & Newcastle's accounts include a historical cost Value Added statement (not reproduced here), which showed that Value Added in the year was £199.8m (£198.1m in previous year)

$$\text{Value Added to sales in 1982 was } \frac{£198.1m}{£620.5m} = 0.32$$

$$\text{in 1983 was } \frac{£199.8m}{£641.8m} = 0.31$$

Current cost value added was not disclosed

Value Added to payroll costs
The Value Added statement also disclosed that payroll costs were £128.2m (£130.6m in previous year).
Therefore the historical cost Value Added to payroll was

$$1982 \quad \frac{£198.1m}{£130.6m} = 1.52$$

$$1983 \quad \frac{£199.8m}{£128.2m} = 1.56$$

Earnings per share

The accounts of Scottish & Newcastle follow SSAPs 3 and 16 and disclose:

	1983	1982
Historical cost EPS before extraordinary items	9.4p	7.8p
Current cost EPS before extraordinary items	5.1p	3.9p

The historical cost ratio for 1983 was arrived at by dividing the profits before extraordinary items (£26.9m) less the preference dividends (£0.5m) by the 281.8m ordinary shares issued.

The current cost ratio for 1983 was arrived at by dividing the post-tax current cost profit (£14.9m) less the preference dividends (£0.5m) by the 281.8m Ordinary shares issued.

RATIOS MEASURING LIQUIDITY, SOLVENCY AND FINANCIAL STRUCTURE

Current ratio

Current assets on the historical cost basis, divided by current liabilities:

$$1982 \ : \ \frac{£154.7m}{£135.6m} = 1.14$$

$$1983 \ : \ \frac{£153.5m}{£134.6m} = 1.14$$

The same ratio calculated on a current cost basis produces a slightly different result because the stocks, which form part of the numerator, are valued at £67.9m rather than at £63.5m:

$$1983 \ : \ \frac{£157.9m}{£134.5m} = 1.17$$

Liquid asset ratio

Constructed as the current ratio, but with stocks omitted from the numerator:

$$1982 \ : \ \frac{£ \ 90.7m}{£135.6m} = 0.67$$

$$1983 \ : \ \frac{£ \ 90.0m}{£134.5m} = 0.67$$

In the above two ratios the denominator includes overdrafts as a component of current liabilities. For Scottish & Newcastle, as for many groups, the distinction between overdrafts and loans is not a real one because the group switches between these alternative sources in accordance with money market opportunities. The ratio user may therefore prefer to rework the above ratios omitting overdrafts from the denominator.

Debtors turnover
During the year debtors rose from £80.7m to £82.4m. The average figure was therefore £81.5m. As turnover was £641.8m, the debtors turnover was

$$\frac{£641.8m}{£\ 81.5m} = 7.9$$

In considering this debtor ratio one factor peculiar to breweries should be kept in mind. Each year the Chancellor of the Exchequer increases the alcohol duties in his Budget, normally in March. Therefore by early May the Scottish & Newcastle balance sheet includes a debtors figure which reflects the price increase which has then been applied for some six weeks. However, the sales figure, against which the debtors are measured, includes about 46 weeks' sales at the old duty rate and about six weeks' sales at the new duty rate. The ratio user who was not aware of this could draw wrong inferences, especially as the duty rises vary from year to year.

Stock turnover
The average historical cost of stock was £63.7m. The average stock at current cost was £68.3m.
Stock turnover on a historical cost basis for 1983 was therefore:

$$\frac{£641.8m}{£\ 63.7m} = 10.1 \text{ times per annum}$$

and on a current cost basis was $\frac{£641.8m}{£\ 68.3m} = 9.4$ times per annum

Gearing
The historical cost gearing, calculated by including preference capital and deferred tax with long term debt was:

in 1982 $\quad \frac{£122.1m}{£437.0m} = 28\%$

in 1983 $\quad \frac{£114.1m}{£442.2m} = 26\%$

The current cost gearing ratio was

in 1983 $\quad \frac{£114.1m}{£520.2m} = 22\%$

As previously mentioned, Scottish & Newcastle switch between overdrafts and loans in accordance with money market opportunities. The ratio user may therefore prefer to include overdrafts (or overdrafts net of cash) in the numerator of the gearing ratio.

Interest cover

Profit before interest and before tax is divided by interest payable.
Using historical cost profit the cover was:

$$\text{in } 1982 \quad \frac{£50.2m}{£18.0m} = 2.8 \text{ times}$$

$$\text{in } 1983 \quad \frac{£54.8m}{£13.7m} = 4.0 \text{ times}$$

Using current cost profit the cover was:

$$\text{in } 1983 \quad \frac{£40.8m}{£13.7m} = 2.98 \text{ times}$$

(This ratio should be as above rather than $\frac{£38.0m}{£10.9m}$ because the latter form of the ratio, which is based on the figures appearing in the current cost profit statement, omits £2.8m of financial income from both numerator and denominator. The £2.8m should be added back to both. It should be added back to current cost operating profit (the numerator) because it goes to swell the available income stream from which interest must be paid. It should be added back to the denominator so that this then shows gross interest payable, rather than a net figure arrived at after setting off the interest receivable).

Further reading on ratio analysis

Foster, G.

Financial statement analysis. Prentice Hall, 1978.
An advanced American text which summarises the research findings on ratios in the projects of Altman, Beaver, Deakin, Edmister, Pinches and others. The references are comprehensive.

Ingham, H. and
  Taylor Harrington, L.

Interfirm comparison. Heinemann, 1980.
A practical book based on British experience of using ratios to compare businesses.

Westwick, C.A.

How to use management ratios. Gower Press, 1973.
A practical British book for managers.